life verse

DISCOVERING THE POWER OF SCRIPTURE IN YOUR STORY

DAVID EDWARDS

*A NavPress resource published in alliance
with Tyndale House Publishers, Inc.*

*For my mom, Dorotha Ann Edwards, for showing me how
to live my life verse and to write about it in the same way*

NAVPRESS⬤®

NavPress is the publishing ministry of The Navigators, an international Christian organization and leader in personal spiritual development. NavPress is committed to helping people grow spiritually and enjoy lives of meaning and hope through personal and group resources that are biblically rooted, culturally relevant, and highly practical.

For more information, visit www.NavPress.com.

Copyright © 2014 by David Edwards. All rights reserved.

A NavPress resource published in alliance with Tyndale House Publishers, Inc.

NAVPRESS and the NAVPRESS logo are registered trademarks of NavPress, The Navigators. Absence of ® in connection with marks of NavPress or other parties does not indicate an absence of registration of those marks.

TYNDALE is a registered trademark of Tyndale House Publishers, Inc.

ISBN 978-1-61291-638-5

Cover design by Ron Kaufmann

Cover photograph copyright © IsaacLKoval/iStockphoto. All rights reserved.

Some of the anecdotal illustrations in this book are true to life and are included with the permission of the persons involved. All other illustrations are composites of real situations, and any resemblance to people living or dead is coincidental.

Cataloging-in-Publication Data is Available.

Printed in the United States of America

20	19	18	17	16	15	14
7	6	5	4	3	2	1

"This book is a masterful study of an important but neglected subject: the importance of the 'life verse' in the Christian life. My heart burned within me as I moved from chapter to chapter. I wish I had read a book like this decades ago. *Life Verse* is a remarkable blending of biblical truth and practical counsel. Young believers and veteran Christians will both benefit from reading this book. I got so caught up in *Life Verse* that I read it in one sitting! May the Lord use this book to help revive His needy church."

Warren W. Wiersbe, former pastor of Moody Church, author of the Be Series of Bible studies

"Dave has been a friend for years and is one of the most effective communicators I know. He's passionate, creative, direct, and hilarious. Dave has a unique way of helping you understand complex biblical truths in a simple, digestible way. In this important book, Dave will guide you prayerfully toward discovering a verse from the Bible to help guide your decisions, direct your path, and define your future. My life verse is Acts 20:24."

Craig Groeschel, lead pastor of LifeChurch.tv

"David Edwards is one of the best teachers I know. He has mastered the art of bringing the Word alive in an engaging way that offers practical solutions for everyday living. *Life Verse* is a wonderful approach to the personal application of God's promises for your life. Transformation is inevitable."

Michelle McKinney Hammond, author of *Right Attitudes for Right Living*

"One word from God can make all the difference. Perhaps this is nowhere more true than when God uses one passage of Scripture to direct and guide our lives. In these pages David Edwards helps you discover your life verse as well as encouragement and hope for your future. My life verse is Isaiah 43:1-4."

Margaret Feinberg, author of *Wonderstruck*

"The Scriptures have inspired some of the greatest verses of my life and music. Dave and I have been friends for a long time; he and his book are for real. Dave's writing is easy to follow, friendly, compassionate, engaging, and motivating; his stories are great, and I always enjoy his humor. *Life Verse* is a clever, creative, yet practical book. It unlocks the value of finding your story in God's Story. This book will help you discover your life verse."

Bart Millard, lead singer of MercyMe

"In *Life Verse*, David Edwards shows us how influential even one verse from God's holy Word can be in transforming your life. I learned a lot reading this book and highly recommend it!"

Kylie Bisutti, author of *I'm No Angel*

"David Edwards is one of my favorite speakers and writers. And *Life Verse* is like a bolt of lightning. It heightens your senses, illuminates the darkness, and changes the situation. In this day and age of noise and chatter, it is imperative that we all discover and share our story. This is what makes you *you*. *Life Verse* uses the grid of Scripture to help us clarify and redefine who we really are. My life verse is Matthew 6:33. This book is a must-read for all who are serious about impacting this generation."

Dr. Jay Strack, president and founder of Student Leadership University

"Whether in the pulpit or on the page, David Edwards is one of the most effective communicators I know. David's practical, biblically grounded wisdom and personal example will help you discover the power of Scripture in your story. Your life verse will adjust the way you see yourself and the world around you. My life verse is Proverbs 20:7. Read this book—it will lift you up."

Dr. Johnny M. Hunt, senior pastor of First Baptist Woodstock, Woodstock, GA

"My friend David Edwards has served us well with this book. In a style all his own, he takes some ancient practices that have shaped the lives of Jesus' followers for centuries and brings a freshness of language and insight to them. David acts as a wise guide on this journey of interacting with the truth of the Scriptures so that we don't miss the point: to see, know, and love God. My life verse is 1 Timothy 1:15-16."

Jerry Gillis, lead pastor of The Chapel, Getzville, NY

"David Edwards knows the best story is the one whose life is contained in God's story. *Life Verse* helps you discover the landmark in your own spiritual story. As you embark on the journey of looking for your life verse, David helps you mine for gold in finding your spiritual treasure. I wish I would have had this book forty years ago when I was digging for my life verse. David is right—there is power in Scripture in your story. My life verse has been John 3:30."

Ken Whitten, senior pastor of Idlewild Baptist Church, Lutz, FL

"In *Life Verse*, David Edwards has focused the spotlight on the absolute necessity of absorbing the Word of God into your life. This book will be a tool in changing your perspective, your attitude, and your life as it equips you to address every situation with Scripture and to unite your pursuits with God's direction. My life verse is Romans 1:16."

Alex Himaya, lead pastor of theChurch.at, Tulsa, OK

"I've known David Edwards a long time. The people described in this book achieved their potential as they found their life verse! You can be one of those people if you read and apply the great insight found in these pages. David has helped me, and he will do the same for you. God has a life verse for you. Happy hunting as you read *Life Verse*; you'll never be the same."

Dr. Chris Stephens, lead pastor of Faith Promise Church, Knoxville, TN

CONTENTS

Acknowledgments   vii

Introduction: The Power of One Verse   ix

Part I: **Re-Verse: Trading Our Old Stories**
CHAPTER 1   Listen to Your Life   7
CHAPTER 2   Inventory Your Story   25
CHAPTER 3   When Stories Collide   33
CHAPTER 4   Outgrow Your Story   49

Part II: **Well-Versed: The World of the Life Verse**
CHAPTER 5   What Your Life Verse Is Not   65
CHAPTER 6   The Power of Your Life Verse   77
CHAPTER 7   The Birth of a Life Verse   91
CHAPTER 8   The Ultimate Life Verse   103

Part III: **Chapter and Verse: Reading for Your Life Verse**
CHAPTER 9   How Do You Read?   123
CHAPTER 10   The Way of the Ear   135
CHAPTER 11   The Pop of the Page   157

Part IV: **Uni-Verse: Discovering Your Life Verse**
CHAPTER 12   Anatomy of a Life Verse   179
CHAPTER 13   Roaming the Neighborhood   187
CHAPTER 14   Taking the Life Verse Journey   201
CHAPTER 15   Living with Your Life Verse   213

ACKNOWLEDGMENTS

THE DISCOVERY of a life verse is a grateful, joyous journey for each believer. Only God can reveal the life verse to an individual. But if I were going to give a life verse to the ones who have shared the time, conversation, and prayers that have contributed the content of this book, I would choose John 15:15: "I have called you friends."

Toni Richmond: Before one word was put on a page, you listened faithfully to me dream out loud about this book and offered holy feedback that deepened and broadened my understanding of the life verse.

Tarina (Taquina Tamina Taweena Doreena) Briggs: Your contribution was amazing. Thank you for your help and friendship.

Dr. Brian Snell, Elena, and Olivia: Thank you for your gift of the electronic tablet; this was my first book written without pen and paper and the reason I made my deadline. Thank you for the late-night technology troubleshooting. If you ever decide not to practice medicine, you've got a career in tech support.

Bishop Tony Miller: I will always be thankful you saw past my homeless attire and extended your friendship. Thank you for all the shared meals in which the main course was the work of God. The words you've shared with me always bring life to my spirit.

Brian Thomasson: For seeing the big picture and believing in the importance of each person discovering their life verse.

Brian Smith: For your careful and meticulous reading of the manuscript, bringing discerning changes and thoughtfully improving the material in endlessly helpful ways. Most of all, your encouragement kept my focus and my words fresh.

Dr. Richard Hogue: For the extraordinary gift of your friendship, and all the early-morning conversations along my years of writing. I will never forget when you said to me, "You can write." Those words were fuel for my soul. Who knew that I'd have a Harvard graduate reading my manuscript?

To all those who read this book, begin a new story by discovering their life verse, and courageously believe it, act on it, and through living the life verse bless others. Thank you.

The Power of One Verse

CAN ONE VERSE from the Bible really change your life? Yes. Yes it can.

Life can be repetitive and often predictable. We get into our deep ruts, and it can become hard to see out over the edges with truth and fresh perspective. But the right verse can cut through the fog of routine, low-level living.

The power of a well-chosen verse can change, convict, confront, and cleanse. A verse can liberate, empower, deliver, reenergize, and reorient to a way of seeing and living. Word by word, line by line, the holy sentences change the nature and direction of present events. Long-believed personal limitations are left in the dust, negative patterns are dismantled, and the heart and mind are awakened to new possibilities.

A verse that changes your life? It's not a new idea. God's followers throughout history have been familiar with the phenomenon.

Followers like Martin Luther, who found a verse that would not only change his life but would alter the course of history. He read Romans 1:17, "The righteous man shall live by faith," and saw that salvation and righteous living were a gift God offered with no strings attached. The local church of his day taught that works and sacraments were also necessary for righteousness before God, so Luther wrote his Ninety-Five Theses, a bold act that triggered the Protestant Reformation.

Followers like William Wilberforce, who read Galatians 3:28, where Paul declared, "There is neither Jew nor Greek, there is neither slave nor free man, . . . for you are all one in Christ Jesus." These words weighed heavy on his heart, to the point where he fought to abolish the slavery that had become so deeply embedded in the culture and economy of the British Empire.

Followers like Fanny Crosby, who lost her sight at six weeks of age but held on to 1 John 3:2: "Beloved, now we are children of God, and . . . when He appears, we will be like Him, because we will see Him just as He is." She saw Jesus with the eyes of her heart, writing some of the most glorious hymns of modern-day Christianity.

Followers like William Cary, who took Mark 16:15 to heart ("Go into all the world and preach the gospel to all creation") and spent forty-one years as a missionary to India, laying the foundation for nine translations of the Bible, advocating for education and social reform, and inspiring countless other missionaries after him.

Followers like Dr. Bill Bright, a businessman shaped by Matthew 28:19: "Go therefore and make disciples of all the nations." This verse inspired Dr. Bright to start Campus Crusade for Christ and to write a gospel booklet that has become one of the most widely used tools in evangelism around the world.

Billy Graham. Romans 5:8: "While we were yet sinners, Christ died for us." His ministry has shared this message all over the globe.

Heidi Baker. Matthew 5:3: "Blessed are the poor in spirit, for theirs is the kingdom of heaven." Orphan children are fed, clothed, and sheltered.

Dawson Trotman. Second Timothy 2:2: "Entrust these to faithful men who will be able to teach others also." He began the ministry known as The Navigators; people all over the world have been discipled because he let one verse shape his life.

You get the idea. Of course, all of these people read and lived the whole Bible, but each of them discovered one verse that served as a frame, a guide for each unique life. A single verse has the power to change a life and, in so doing, to change the world. No one doubts that what God accomplished through these people—and through millions of other God-followers—He accomplished through the power of Scripture. Each with a life verse firmly fixed, these people made God-honoring choices, overcame incredible odds, persevered, and rose above the challenges of sameness to accomplish the will of God. In each case, the voice of God in Scripture broke through.

When we take a verse seriously, it creates profound change in our reality, it taps into creative resources of faith, it welcomes bold imagination, it fosters new compassion for the hurts of others, it opens us up to the help of God's Spirit, and it surprises us with confidence that God is our future.

The way of the future lies in reaching back. Back to the rich texts of Scripture, back into the world of God's Word. Then we rediscover God's Word, and we hear it speaking from the world in which it was written, into the world we now inhabit. A life verse helps us look at our world from God's perspective.

The purpose of this book is to assist you in the process of reading and hearing the Word of God, to help you to reach back into the world of God's Word to discover your life verse for living in this world.

I make a distinction between *finding* and *discovering* a life verse. While I was researching, I found many websites that presented pages of Scripture and encouraged believers to pick a verse they liked. Clicking and picking is not the focus of this book. Rather, this book will help you read the Bible with a receptive heart, and out of that reading God will speak, and you will discover the life verse He has chosen for you.

This book is presented in four parts. In Part I, "Re-Verse: Trading Our Old Stories," we confront the stories that began at the earliest moments of our lives and have given us identity. The stories we choose to live are our attempt to make sense of traumatic and difficult events. Our stories come fully equipped with the promise that we will be safe and loved. As we grow up, it becomes evident that we are emotionally, physically, or spiritually stuck in an old story; we have in fact been living out a death sentence. Discovering your life verse begins by recognizing your old story and realizing that God has a new one for you to live. Your life verse serves as the opening line of your new story.

Part II, "Well-Versed: The World of the Life Verse," explains what your life verse will do for you—and what it won't. This section introduces and expands on several important life verses: What do we learn from the life verse of the nation Israel? How does the birth of Mary's life verse help us understand how to find ours? What about Jesus—what was His life verse? I'll also let you in on my life verse and how it found me.

Part III, "Chapter and Verse: Reading for Your Life Verse," is about sitting down and opening up the pages of Scripture to let it infiltrate our souls, which requires us to tune our hearts and souls. Life comes to us through the pages—life that becomes real to us as we read the Bible humbly and expectantly. Reading Scripture brings us into the world of God.

Part IV is "Uni-Verse: Discovering Your Life Verse." Knowing where to begin can seem like a daunting task. Thankfully, finding your life verse is not all up to you. In this section I'll unpack how the help of the Spirit brings insight and understanding as you read Scriptures, so you can discover and live out your life verse.

Along the way I've provided a few questions here and there to help you think through and apply the principles of this book. You'll also find, in chapters 12–14, a personal inventory that will help you discover and explore your life verse.

Read on, take the information to heart, and begin the journey of discovering your life verse. I recommend you take time with each chapter, digest the truth it contains, and let the Lord challenge, stretch, and lead you through the discovery process.

PART I

RE-VERSE: TRADING OUR OLD STORIES

THE ATMOSPHERE backstage at Christian music events is not like being backstage at a typical rock concert. Instead of drugs, alcohol, or groupies, you find fruit, water, and a tray of Chick-fil-A, while amiable musicians sit quietly disengaged from their surroundings, staring into their laptops as they place bids on cool gear on eBay.

Which made the man standing backstage at this particular show even more conspicuous. I made a casual inventory and noticed he was five foot eleven, a solid 230 pounds, with long salt-and-pepper hair and an even longer beard to match. He sported a black leather vest with a brown cross embroidered across its back, worn over a plaid shirt, completed with well-traveled jeans and boots. He was terminally cool. He could've been anything from a rock star to a hit man.

He also had a wallet on a chain, just like mine. Fascinated, I pointed to it.

"Hey, cool wallet," I said, pulling mine from my back pocket.

He smiled warmly. "Oh, nice," he said.

By this point I figured there was a motorcycle in this guy's life. "What do you ride?" I asked.

"A black Harley Electra Glide," he said enthusiastically, extending his hand. "I'm Jim Gillespie."

Jim's welcoming countenance made it obvious that he loved Jesus, so I briefly introduced myself, then asked him, "What do you do?"

"I'm pastor of men's ministry at Richland Creek Community Church."

I was surprised. "What?" I said. "But where's your golf shirt with embroidered church logo?"

We laughed, and then Jim told me his story:

I grew up in an abusive home. My alcoholic dad had been in and out of prison for most of his life, and he regularly beat my mom. She moved us to a little town called West Grove, near Lancaster, Pennsylvania. It didn't take long to figure out that I could do whatever I wanted; by eighth grade I was already drinking and smoking pot. From there I escalated to doing cocaine, LSD, and meth, and dealing drugs. By tenth grade I'd been expelled. At seventeen I was living with my pregnant girlfriend; by eighteen I was a single dad working odd jobs and selling drugs.

Into these dark days shone a ray of hope. I met

my wife, Laurie, and we moved to Texas. She inspired me to attempt to live right, but my habits were stronger than my desire, and it didn't take long for me to turn back to my selfish ways. I started staying out late and drinking. I had become like my dad.

I still remember the night Laurie told me I was the most hateful person she had ever met. I knew she was right and told her if I were her, I'd leave me.

She raised her voice: "Lucky for you, God's Word won't let me leave you! So I'm staying and I'll be praying for you."

Old habits die hard—I went from bad to worse, joining a motorcycle gang called The Scorpions. I would leave for days, drinking, partying, and spending all our money—

I interrupted him. "A motorcycle gang?"

He nodded and continued:

You have to be bad to be in one. Well, I was so bad they made me leave! You know you're really bad when thieves and drug dealers tell you to get out. Like a bike with no brakes, I was headed downhill. I spent the next two years in depression and rarely left the house.

I found Laurie's Bible and began reading through the Gospels. I read every day, page by page, verse by verse. Like a scalpel, God's Word peeled back the layers of my life until I saw myself for who I really was: a liar, a drunk, a drug addict, a thief, and a stranger to my own family.

Then I read about a woman who loved much because she'd been forgiven much. I knew I had plenty I needed to be forgiven for. I kept reading every day until I read about a thief next to Jesus who was saved at the last minute. The Spirit brought that story to life for me: I was that thief, dying a criminal's death.

The gospel flooded my mind, and I stood to my feet and cried out to God, "If You'll take me just the way I am, You can have me from this day forward! I'm all Yours."

That was the day Jesus saved this renegade and outlaw.

I continued reading the Bible. I read Acts and got involved in church and connected with a mentor. Then I read Romans, and that's where God gave me a verse to memorize and meditate on, a verse that gave shape to my life and ministry.

What is it? There in our backstage conversation Jim pushed up his shirtsleeve, stretched out his right arm, and showed me a tattoo of two characters, each a little smaller than a playing card. They were the numbers 5:8. Jim's life verse is Romans 5:8: "God demonstrates His own love toward us, in that while we were yet sinners, Christ died for us."

✦   ✦   ✦

We'd like to hear your story. Please visit YourLifeVerse.org and share how you discovered your life verse and how the Lord has worked through it in your life.

CHAPTER 1

Listen to Your Life

YOUR LIFE is saying something to you.

Jim Gillespie's story is the perfect illustration of the way each of us can trade in an old story for a new one. A choice is set before each one of us: We can choose to live a story that, in the end, will kill us and everything else that is good about our lives. Or we can choose life.

Like Jim, you can discover within the pages of Scripture a perspective-changing, direction-focusing verse for your life. That's what happened for Rick Barry, my friend and youth pastor at Keystone Fellowship in Souderton, Pennsylvania:

> When I was a senior in high school, my senior pastor challenged me to not just read my Bible, but to get to know God's heart behind each book of the Bible. He challenged me to read and study a book of the Bible

each day for an entire month. I started off with the book of 2 Timothy, and then began to work my way through all of the Epistles.

During my freshman year of college at Michigan State University, I had been praying that God would give me boldness like never before. I wanted to be a light to that campus, and I wanted to make the most of every opportunity that I had to share the gospel. However, I continually found myself intimidated by my peers and (in my mind) their lack of desire to hear about the things of God. One day, I had a clear chance to bring up Christ in a conversation with my friend but completely chickened out. I let fear get the best of me, and I left feeling like a complete failure.

When I got back to my dorm room, I spent time praying. I asked Christ to forgive me and give me the strength not to miss out on any more opportunities like that again. I then opened up my Bible to read the book of Philippians for the day; I'd been reading this one book over and over for three months. Before I began reading I simply prayed, "God, show me something today to help me have boldness so that You will be glorified." As I read through chapter 1, I came across Philippians 1:21, which I had underlined. But this time as I was reading, God opened my eyes to Philippians 1:20, which is a prayer that Paul prayed for himself. For the first time, it popped out at me. The verse says:

I eagerly expect and hope that I will in no way
be ashamed, but will have sufficient courage so
that now as always Christ will be exalted in my
body, whether by life or by death. (*NIV*)

My eyes were opened to the vulnerability in Paul's
prayer, and I began to pray that for myself. I prayed
it when I was in my dorm, on the bus, in class, at
parties. I prayed it everywhere. As months passed, I
was still praying that for myself. I came to realize that
Philippians 1:20 was not just a verse that I wanted
to be true while I was in college, but I wanted it to
be true for all my life. I realized that wherever I was,
whatever I was doing, whenever I was doing it, I
never wanted to be ashamed, but I wanted sufficient
courage so that Christ would be exalted in my life,
whether by life or by death.

My life verse is the prayer that God showed me,
which I continually pray and want to be true for
my life!

What's your story? Maybe it's one in which every day seems
filled with the same struggles. Get up, get ready, go to work,
go home, go to bed—only to start the cycle all over again.
Feeling trapped in life, people look for distraction—something to numb the pain, a way to get away from it all. But
this only creates more frustration. Avoiding life's struggles is
not the answer.

Life can sometimes feel like a hamster's journey on his

wheel. During these times it's quite easy to drift off into fantasy, dreaming about all the different ways we might achieve happiness, running mental video clips of better circumstances and more loving people. All those images and dreams have a way of cluttering our heads, bogging us down with so many pseudo-options that we don't know what to do next. We begin to feel like there is no way out.

We are capable of making a new choice to see life as a gift, starting a new story in which everything propels us in a positive direction. Jesus acknowledged, "In this world you will have trouble." Then He continued, "But take heart! I have overcome the world" (John 16:33, NIV). We will learn much more about this new story later in this book, but first let's muster the courage to take a close look at the old story.

Do joy and contentment seem to elude you? If you've ever felt as though life is unfair, don't blame bad karma or bad luck or even necessarily bad judgment. The real cause is something deeply embedded inside you that governs and directs everything in your life. It's your old story.

I'm not talking about random stories you might share over dinner, but rather your *life* story—the one you tell yourself every moment of every day. There's power in story. How? Let's take a look.

Our Stories Shape Us

John chapter 4 contains many stories, all taking place at the same time. A story of geography and the division of people. Another story encompassing history, the present, and the future. Stories both natural and supernatural, religious and theological. Stories of racism, gender, and politics. And centrally interwoven throughout all of these is a story of a conversation between a man and a woman. On the surface these two individuals are very different, but something beautiful is unfolding, involving more than can be observed by onlookers.

The story begins with Jesus sitting at Jacob's well, outside a Samaritan village. It's high, shadowless noon. Jesus is hot, road weary, and thirsty, and He has nothing with which to draw water. So He waits.

He hears footsteps, hurried and hesitant. He looks up, then down, then does a double take at the woman preparing to draw water. She is used to being stared at by men; she's beautiful—she has always looked ten years younger than her age—she knows it . . . and she doesn't care. Any illusions she used to believe have now been shattered. She has enjoyed the glamorous life, been wined and dined by well-to-do men, heard her share of empty promises, and reached out to the men she thought would bring her happiness. On closer examination, Jesus sees cynicism in her eyes, along with a sadness revealing that the best of her days are now behind her. She expects nothing more from life than what it gives her now. Her stories—they are many, all marred by failure—have shaped the life she now lives.

Our stories tell us who we are. They teach us about the world in which we live and how that world works. Patterns that are repeated over and over in our young experience become the plotlines for the decades that follow. Messages that we hear—or that we interpret from what we hear—become the infallible maxims in which we place our faith. Our stories powerfully determine who we become and how we value ourselves.

We often trade away the true story for tales others have told us, stories that we believe simply because they're familiar, even if they're painful, even when they've grown stale. We easily buy the stories we grew up believing, the ones that made false promises about what would bring us love. When we live a story we were never meant to live, we find ourselves stuck emotionally, spiritually—even physically. We feel powerless to make any changes, so we cling even more to the old story as our excuse for not moving forward.

The simple truth? You are who you are because of the story you have believed about yourself. If you are tired of the way things are and you want to begin a new story, you must be willing to break out of the old one.

Our Stories Shelter Us

She has learned the hard way that everything comes
with a price tag. Maybe she has given every man to
whom she has joined herself the benefit of the doubt,
always finding a way to blame herself. Stories have a
way of helping us hide from others and from ourselves.

She shows up at the well at the time of day when
no one else would be there. Maybe she doesn't want
to hear the whispers of other women gossiping among

themselves about her. Maybe she doesn't want to be reminded of her past behavior, of those five failed relationships. She manages life by trying not to let loneliness get the best of her. She tries not to look at the consequences of her choices. But choices have a way of catching up to us, and somebody has to pay. The mistakes of this beautiful woman by the well have accumulated. She pays the price for them every day.

We use stories to inoculate us from pain we've experienced, to create something beautiful from the difficult and traumatic events of our lives, to explain the moments when the most important people of our lives would not or could not meet our need to be loved. Whether it's a huge tragedy like losing a parent or suffering abuse, or something less significant, we just don't want to hurt, so we build a story for shelter. Some people assume that experiencing pain is a sign that something is wrong, so they do whatever they can to avoid feeling more pain—and by extension they attempt to prevent the "something wrong"—not realizing the pain is a sign that the story is breaking down. Truth is trying to invade.

There are many things people reach for: pills, makeup, shopping, booze. Our society offers a lot of creative options for hiding and anesthetizing pain, trying to convince us that these opiates will make us better and happier. But these quick fixes don't work, because they are external, temporal solutions to an internal and eternal problem. "There is a way which seems right to a man," wrote wise Solomon, "but its end is the way of death" (Proverbs 14:12).

Hiding under a story is a means of avoiding pain without confronting the problem. Although we manage to numb the ache, we also miss the opportunity to be free. As long as we sit in the shelter of our old stories, those stories will feed us a steady diet of lies about why we are or are not lovable or acceptable. They will craft false scenarios pointing the finger of blame for our pain.

Our Stories Speak to Us

Over the years, our minds have a way of condensing our stories down to pithy slogans that play over and over in our thoughts. This unnamed woman at the well has lived five stories, each with a different man, and all those stories have been reduced to one line: "Shame on you; you've failed at love." This theme has taken on its own voice, speaking constantly to her, forcing her to live and relive her loss and regret.

Jesus sees her and speaks to her. She is used to watching men nervously fumble around for the right words to gain her attention. Not so with Jesus. He's completely at ease, unfazed by her beauty. He speaks to her comfortably, as though to a friend on the same social stratum. Jesus speaks first. He doesn't try using any worn-out pickup lines, like, "I don't think I've seen you at this well before." Instead He asks her for water. By asking her for a favor, He is putting her at ease. He knows from the start that she has chosen her timing in order to avoid people. He looks past all the obstacles. Race, religion, reputation. Jesus never lets differences make a difference.

She questions how a Jewish man can risk talking to a Samaritan woman, asking her for water, putting Himself at the mercy of a foreign woman. Rather than explain to her that He doesn't care about their ethnic or religious differences, He says if only she knew who is asking her for a drink, she would ask and He would give her living water. Jesus is trying to startle her out of her trance—the mind-numbing, hope-stealing, repetitious buzzing voice of her past stories—to get beneath the surface facade by making her think.

Something inside tells her that Jesus isn't talking about water drawn with a bucket. A new voice has interrupted the old voice, and she is beginning to be stirred.

"Living water? What do you mean?"

This woman knows men and their ways; this is no pickup line. Her soul begins to open. She realizes that while she has been talking about water drawn from a well, this Jewish teacher is speaking of "water" from God.

Although our defining stories happened long ago, we still hear them in our thoughts, echoing back and forth, down through the haunted halls of our experience. We feel the shock waves of these past stories in our present relationships; we experience the plotlines in our current situations. Often today's conflicts are driven by our stories from an era long past.

If you want to become aware of the influence of your old story, here's a good place to start: Think about the last twenty-four hours. The conversation you had with your boss, your spouse, your sibling, or even yourself. Think about something you did that made you feel terrible about yourself. Was there a moment when your emotions were off the chart, when you flipped out or melted down? Have the tension and conflict inside you escalated and spilled out onto those around you? Have you heard yourself shouting, silently or aloud, "What's wrong with everybody?"

These are all indications that you were playing an old story. Whether you thought about it in that moment or not, your story was speaking to you.

It's important to remember that your story will repeat itself. It will come in different forms—through varied characters and settings—but what you feel and how you react are the same. Even after all these years, your old story is re-created, resurfaced, retold.

Our Stories Can Be Switched

The woman realizes how thirsty she has always been.
She has been thirsty for something that neither men,
nor money, nor sex could ever give. Jesus is way
ahead of her. From the moment she walked up to
the well, Jesus has known how desperately she has
searched for someone or something to satisfy her.
She has thirsted for a better life, for a new start, for a
fuller way of living.
She has been drinking polluted water.

"Okay, I'd like some of this water you're advertising."

"Wonderful," replies Jesus. "Bring your husband, and we'll all talk about it."

Busted. "I . . . I don't have a husband." She can't look Him in the eye.

"That's right. And you're not married to the man you're living with now."

Her heart skips a beat. "How . . . oh, I see, you must be a prophet!" A seer who knows her whole life history. Suddenly her secrets are exposed. This is getting too close.

But her thirst for authentic life won't let her simply walk away. She can't bear another day with an empty heart. Even though this man knows her inside out, she feels no judgment or condemnation in His presence. Maybe He could show her the way out of the maze of her old stories.

Problem: She and God have not been on speaking terms for a while. Of course, she still knows how to talk religion. Religion has had its benefits in her life, allowing her to cover her true condition with a layer of ritual, setting up buffers that have kept others at a distance. If religion is what the Jewish teacher wants, she can accommodate. She searches her memory and comes up with one of the perennial hot topics: "Our fathers worshipped on this mountain, but you Jews say the Jerusalem temple is the only place of true worship."

But Jesus recognizes the ploy for what it is—her old story's last effort to maintain control by creating a smoke screen, a distraction from the woman's deepest needs. Gently He engages her, continuing to bring her back to her need for the new story that God can give her through His Spirit—the new life for which she had given up all hope.

Finally she acknowledges, "I know that Messiah is coming."

And Jesus, gaze of love unwavering, begins her new story: "I who speak to you am He."

She finds herself suddenly awake. The change for which she has longed is no longer a distant hope but now a present reality. In that moment she closes the book on her stories of shame, regret, and loss, and she turns the page to a story of new life. Her secrets lose their power; the honesty is refreshing, airing her soul. Where she has always before lived in uncertainty and doubt, she finds herself now unflinchingly confident.

She can't keep it in. She has to tell someone! Forgetting her original errand, leaving her water pot behind, she sprints for the town. "You all know me, what I've been all my life. But I've met the Messiah, and look at me now!"

It's never too late to start your new story.

What story is keeping you from liking yourself? Keeping you from loving others? What's robbing you of peace, contentment, and freedom? Keeping you from enjoying the people in your life and receiving your life as a gift? As you find the answer to these questions, you'll run into good news: *You are capable of change.*

It's never too late to switch your story.

When we decide to move beyond our old, self-destructive, self-limiting stories and switch to God's eternal story, we find who we *really* are. We become strong and rooted. We become more complete, no longer defined merely by pain and loss. Yes, pain is still in our lives, but we are no longer dominated by it, able instead to experience the joy of God, to connect to His presence, to enjoy real intimacy. A new story brings strength, courage, power, and freedom to live the gift of life God has given us. Paul described it best when he wrote, "We are afflicted . . . but not crushed; perplexed, but not despairing; persecuted, but not forsaken; struck down, but not destroyed" (2 Corinthians 4:8-9).

With a new story, we leave behind our familiar facade and are made real. Real enough to face the disappointment of being defeated. Real enough to face the uncertainties of life without becoming disillusioned. Real enough to face the good, the bad, and everything else without losing hope along the way.

Switching stories is not just a matter of telling ourselves a positive statement. It's an opportunity to live in a whole new reality—God's true reality.

Our Stories Are for Sharing

Before meeting Jesus, her story was one of broken dreams and loss—a story that would leave any listener depressed. But now she has a new story to share: "Is this not the Christ?"

She presents a new perspective, a new way of thinking. Her past serves now only as a springboard to the glorious present and future. One might expect her to return to the town and present a factual case— evidence of Jesus' wisdom and messiahship. Instead she returns to share her story. Like other followers of Jesus, she speaks of what she has seen and heard. She believes, therefore she speaks. Transformed and purified, this woman shares her story, and the people of the city journey out to see and hear Jesus for themselves. She has become a spiritual signpost, showing others the way to find the Messiah.

From the start, Jesus knows that if He wishes, He can walk right into the Samaritan village and start preaching. But He chooses to wait outside the village, there to change the story of one nameless woman, who then runs to tell other nameless Samaritans. Because of her story they come and see and hear and touch Jesus for themselves, and over the next two days an undisclosed number come to faith in Jesus as Messiah. Scripture says they are "many."

Jesus could have introduced Himself, but He chose instead to set a life on fire and let others be drawn to its light. Because the woman shared her story, the good news spread beyond the boundaries of Judaism long before the time of the apostles, and the early church reached out from Jerusalem. Jesus

Himself—through a nameless woman—opened the doors of salvation to the rest of the world.

Because she shared.

In any given city, there are thousands of stories assembled, each different, yet all the same—everyone thirsty for something more. So many people drawing from wells that cannot quench the heart's thirst. For so many it would only take one person to share the way to the living water.

Stories aren't just the relaying of facts. They're not just words. They come through the eyes, facial expressions, posture, tone of voice, and energy. The story is told and retold in the streets, in cubicles, in break rooms, in schools, homes, and churches. And beside wells. And every time a truly new story is told, you'll find Jesus the Messiah at the center of it—the Savior, the God who loves the brokenhearted.

In fact, I'd like to offer you an opportunity to share your life verse story. When you've discovered your life verse, please visit YourLifeVerse.org and tell me how it happened and how the Lord has used your verse in your life.

Old becomes new. Lost is found. Hurts are healed. Not by the sharing of an idea, but by the power of the gospel, conveyed through someone's personal experience of faith in Jesus. Now that's a story worth sharing.

Our Stories Have a Start

Even now that she has met the Messiah and committed her life to Him, her past sometimes haunts her. Those words of Jesus still sting: "Go call your husband." Like a poker taken from the flames, they can still sear her heart when the memory catches her off guard. He laid bare her personal life—all the stories, all the unhappy endings. She'd never planned for so much domestic disorder. Her thoughts race back to the young boy whose bride she'd first become. The increasing distance, the fights, the separation, the affairs.

But in spite of the fresh flood of pain, she is grateful that Jesus surfaced her not-so-hidden history. Like a doctor draining a festering wound, He has begun the healing process by identifying the central problem. As though He were saying, "If you want a new story, here's where you have to start."

And so her shame has turned into a shout: "Come and see the man who told me everything." The facts of her past life are the same. But now they are bathed in the cleansing light of a brand-new story.

Just as the Samaritan woman could now tell a new story with a new opening line, so it is with us. The facts of our pasts don't just disappear; we've all lived the lives we've lived, and neither we nor God slip into a state of denial over what's happened. Instead the eternal words of Jesus begin to fill the pages of our stories. His words change our perspective and purpose. You need a new opening line—one that gives the old facts a new theme.

Every story starts somewhere. Stories have opening lines, like "Once up on a time." Opening lines set the tone for what is to follow. So during this journey of discovery, think of your life verse as the opening line to your new story. Your old story began with an opening line written by others. But God is the author of your life verse, and the rest of your new story.

> *How do you see yourself in the story of the woman at the well?*

> *When you share your story, does it affect your listeners positively or negatively?*

> *What aspects of your story have not turned out as you hoped?*

> *Have you ever surprised yourself by saying or doing things you thought you never would? Please explain.*

> *At this moment write your opening line of your story.*

CHAPTER 2

Inventory Your Story

I WAS once scheduled to speak at a conference in Philadelphia, so I flew in a few days early to enjoy the city. The weather was not particularly good—cold and rainy—but it made the landmarks seem majestic and mysterious.

Someone had mentioned a specific restaurant to me, and since I'm a fan of food, I decided to find the place. Turns out it was a bit outside the city. I drove. And drove. After a while I realized I was *way* out of the city. I didn't know there were back roads in Philadelphia, but there are, and I think I found all of them. These were not just back roads—they felt like roads that had been abandoned.

Then I saw the light. No, not from heaven—from a mini-mart. *I'll stop to get directions*, I thought. And I turned across the lane into the parking lot. Now I discovered there were more lights—pretty blue and red flashing lights.

I wanted to get out of the way of the police car, so I drove through the parking lot and around the gas pumps. Somehow I was still in its way. I took one more lap . . . then I realized those lights were meant for me.

I knew I hadn't been speeding, because I could barely see for the rain. Everything inside of me felt defensive.

The officer approached my car, so I rolled down the window. "Is there a problem?" I asked.

"Yes," he said. "Did you know you have a traffic cone lodged under your car?"

I got out and looked and, sure enough, there was a bright orange traffic cone sticking out from underneath my car. I'd likely run over it when I drove through a construction zone about four miles earlier, and all the while I had been totally unaware.

This is a worthy word picture for us all. Life provides us with warning signs, telling us that our old stories aren't working. We can ignore the warnings—even drive right over them—but we drag them around with us, and often everyone can see them but us. Meanwhile our stories hinder or stop us from really living.

Not every original story is a negative one. In fact, some of our beginning stories are good. Stories about our personality, our skills, our strengths, our fears, our weaknesses, our habits—all have served a purpose. They've made sense of the order and joy, as well as the chaos and disappointment in our lives; they've given us permission for the choices we've made. Most of the time, we've been completely unaware of our stories, but there comes a time when we do have to consciously acknowledge what's going on within us. We have to learn how to recognize and perhaps rewrite the driving influence of these stories.

This is not as easy as it sounds, because for so long our stories have been a place of safety and have protected us from the events that were too much to bear. They have brought us comfort when there was none elsewhere. This chapter contains a series of questions to help inventory your story—the courageous entry point into this intimidating process.

Where Did Your Story Start?

We touched on this in the last chapter, but it bears repeating: We've been taught to avoid pain at all cost. Our culture doesn't like pain, to the point that entire industries and marketing plans are built on helping us avoid pain. Because of this pattern of avoidance, we grow up hearing and thinking thoughts like:

> *I can't deal with this—I'm leaving.*
> *This is not happening now.*
> *I shouldn't have to feel this way.*
> *I need something to make the pain stop.*
> *I'm such a wreck—I should just stop trying.*
> *What's wrong with me?*

In other words, pain = bad, pleasure = good.

Even if the message to you was "Be a big boy (or girl) and take it," you had to figure out a story that would help you "take it," because, doggone it, it hurt!

So the years pass and we do our best to keep the pain and the struggle from invading our conscious awareness. But working so hard to avoid our pain is what derails us from the best track; it's hard emotional work, the opposite of peace. The irony is that the road to freedom and maturity goes *through* our messes and hurts, not around them.

Feeling and expressing rage, disappointment, hate, or hurt don't make us weird or weak—they mean that the story we have told ourselves for so long, the poisonous plotlines we've been living, are no longer working. By being willing to face the pain, we claim God's promise that His infinite power is there to transform the old story. God works in the midst of our painful stories to free us from old, self-destructive ways. He alone gives us the ability to trade our old story for a new story.

Have You Left God Out of Your Story?

Some of us have lived with our old stories for so long that nothing else seems able to compete with the false beliefs they created. We've learned to look at our lives as though God either is not involved or is only watching from a distance. Our stories have conditioned us to push God out of our awareness, which is a constant, moment-by-moment effort. The diabolical part is this: Even after we've factored out God, our stories continue to run in the background without our even being aware of it.

But we are living fictional lives, as though our true identity wasn't meant to come from God. These are broken stories. Take a look at this list and consider whether you've ever experienced any of these warning signs:

> *Repeated destructive behavior*
> *Constant fatigue*
> *Explosive, uncontrollable anger*
> *The same toxic patterns repeated in relationships*
> *The sense that nothing is ever good enough*
> *Changing one habit, believing it will solve everything*
> *Thinking that finding the right person to be in love with will make you complete*
> *The belief that you are always paying for every mistake you've made*
> *Feeling empty no matter how good life gets*
> *Never allowing yourself to get close to anyone*
> *Hiding from pain by closing off from self and family*
> *An overwhelming sense of disappointment*
> *A constant feeling of being put down or abandoned*
> *The vain belief that someday it's all gonna change*

This is a short list of signs indicating that we are living stories that have left God out of the picture. The Bible calls this thought pattern "the mind set on the flesh" (Romans 8:6) or "conform[ing] to the pattern of this world" (Romans 12:2, NIV).

What Is Your Old Story Costing You?
Maybe you were once in a relationship where you let the other person see only what you wanted him or her to see. Maybe it seemed like the right thing to do at the time. Or maybe you were in a relationship that worked the other way around: The other person was the one keeping secrets.

When we live with an incomplete story, we suffer a double loss: We lose the people we love, and our perfectly created story takes a beatdown. Although we think our story will protect us, it backfires on us.

Every false story bears a cost; we pay a deep price for conforming our lives to the pattern of this world. When our stories exclude God, then all our actions and choices will be about distracting others away from the real inner me. Our pseudostories rob us of relational connection, of the capacity to grow in knowing both God and others in real ways.

Our stories demand that we continue to hide the real self, lest we suffer rejection. And when our stories backfire, the failure leads us to a choice: Either we keep working to uphold the falsehood and continue to suffer the fallout, or we let the old stories collapse and find a new, better, more powerful, sustaining story—a story that God gives us.

Are You Sick of Your Old Story?

If you're tired of the same old story and are ready for things to change, then it's time to turn the page on your life and genuinely yield to the Spirit in full surrender to Christ. Then we come into several amazing benefits: We are forgiven by God. We are given a new nature and no longer have to be trapped in fictional versions of ourselves. Surrendering to Christ sets us up to receive a whole new story. Our old stories required that we acted, thought, and spoke as though God was not present, and consequently we were "like the surf of the sea, driven and tossed by the wind," as described in James 1:6.

Are You Ready for a New Story?

We must submit and resubmit ourselves in this moment and in every moment that follows. Whatever is going on in your life, take a moment now to begin a prayer that may last a lifetime. Simply say, "God, I'm tired of the old story and I'm ready for a new story." Welcome the presence of God into this moment, and begin to be aware of God's presence in each moment. As these moments add up, you'll discover your life increasingly defined by God's new story.

Are You Ready to Stick By Your New Story?

Learning to live this new story doesn't happen instantly, and it takes effort, but when it happens we find such freedom. Which is why discovering and knowing your life verse is so important. That verse becomes the central kernel around which your new life develops. It's a connecting point to the presence of God, ensuring that you're defined by God rather than by others. You are no longer on the old story's autopilot; rather, you are free to live with your Creator at the helm.

Some things won't change. You still have to face difficulties in life, job, responsibilities, and relationships. But instead of all the thoughts of the day weighing you down, they are now filtered through your life verse and the backdrop of Scripture from which it emerges. Everything you think and feel is now renovated by your life verse.

The only way to dismantle the old story is by continually flooding it with the powerful truth found in your new story, with your life verse at its center. As we saw earlier in this chapter, every false story has a cost; once you begin to live and believe your life verse, the cost of your old story, however big, will seem small compared to the promise of your life verse.

Like a four-by-four truck using all four tires to push its way through the mud, to steadily climb uphill over the rocks and the obstacles, ultimately reaching the top of the mountain—that's how it is with your life verse. It propels you forward, pushes you to make new choices, and pulls you up from the lies and fiction of the past.

Company for the Journey

The old story with its patterns and plotlines has taken up a majority of our time, energy, and choices. The overarching presence of your death sentence must be replaced with a life verse. The negative thinking that has driven our life must be replaced with new words, from the Word of God.

That all sounds good, you say, *but I still feel hopeless and stuck. I don't think I can do it.*

That's the beauty of God's system: You're not alone. God is faithful and will not leave you in an old story—unless you refuse to let go of it. You may think that you're in happy, successful control of your old story—or maybe you think that your old story is hopelessly dominating you. Either way, there will come a moment when your old story collides with the possibility of a new one.

CHAPTER 3

When Stories Collide

EVERY STORY has its own momentum. The longer we live it, the more forceful it becomes. Sometimes a story takes on a life of its own until it's like a runaway train. And you're on board! The story is not always obviously negative; sometimes it's built on success, which has its own pitfalls. It can be hard to believe, but the trappings of success can actually become just that—a trap. Working jobs, making money, paying bills, buying things without any sense of why. We just keep on working, circling sleepily around inside the story until something gets our attention and wakes us up.

Traveling as much as I have over the years, I've seen my share of car crashes, ranging in degree of severity. Some are minor fender benders that are quickly repaired, but then there are more severe collisions and their consequences— mangled, twisted metal, contorted beyond recognition, along with serious bodily injury and lengthy rehabilitation. And what about the life "collisions" that happen without a car: a heart attack, a job loss, an eviction. These and other crashes have a way of causing us to reevaluate life, change our focus, and make new choices.

Collisions are never planned; they are always a shock to the system. Collisions become mental markers of a time when life changed. Just as there are physical collisions, there are also spiritual collisions. These are the result of living on a trajectory of an old story that's gained velocity and finally collides with reality. With truth. With God. In the aftermath we can fight to stay in denial. Or we can accept the moment as an opportunity for change.

It's difficult to imagine a more unlikely convert to Christianity than Saul. Saul was educated under Gamaliel—one of Israel's most distinguished rabbis—and became a radical Jewish zealot who described himself as a Pharisee and a son of a Pharisee, who lived according to the strictest sect of Judaism and was blameless according to the law (see Acts 23:6; Philippians 3:4-6). This young Jewish zealot was so opposed to Christianity that he saw his life's work as the persecution and destruction of what he believed to be a false messianic sect.

He had watched the growth of the Christian faith and perceived it as damaging to his religion; now he was breathing threats and murder against the disciples of Jesus. On his own initiative, Saul went to the high priests and asked for letters to the synagogue at Damascus authorizing him to bring any Christians there back to Jerusalem to be disposed of. (You can read the story in Acts 9.)

Saul terrorized the church, and they feared his rampage against them. But while on the road to Damascus to continue his campaign against the followers of Jesus, Saul got in a collision. No, he didn't rear-end a donkey cart. Rather, Saul's old story of religion, rules, and intolerance had been on a years-long trajectory to collide this day with the risen Savior.

To appreciate the intensity of this collision, it's worth remembering that Saul was convinced Jesus was dead and buried. Now all that was left was for Saul to destroy those who believed in Him. What follows in Saul's story serves as a pattern describing what happens when any of our old stories collide with God's.

So picture the two stories in motion toward their inevitable intersection: Saul's old story of perfectionistic, performance-based living and Jesus' new story of resurrection and redemption. We all know the end result: Saul's life was changed, radically and irrevocably. But it's fascinating to see the process, the pattern of what happens to any of us when our death sentence collides with the life of Jesus. When your old story collides with your new one, you may find yourself going through these same stages.

Crash and Burn

Saul's collision happened around noon, when the sun was at its brightest, which made it all the more startling when a light from heaven suddenly flashed around him—brighter than the noonday sun! Saul fell to the ground and heard a voice saying to him, "Saul, Saul, why are you persecuting

Me?" This was the collision that would change the direction of Saul's life.

Saul, lying flat on his back, dazed and disoriented, cried out, "Who are You, Lord?"

And the answer came blasting back, "I am Jesus whom you are persecuting." Saul had come suddenly face to face with the stark reality that Jesus was not dead but had been resurrected and was seated at the right hand of God. His career as a religious bully had instantly come undone.

When stories collide, there's a moment of dawning awareness, when our old stories become recognizable for what they are, and it's suddenly hard to believe we've lived with such toxic falsehood for so long. Like Saul, many live with a religious mind-set, believing love from God is earned or increases if they behave correctly. If we've lived with the belief that we are only as good as our performance, a collision brings us to the truth: Living life as a pass/fail performance means we will never feel as though we measure up. The lie melts before our eyes when we realize that God's acceptance is given, not earned.

A collision with the presence of Jesus turns our most cherished beliefs inside out, initiating a paradigm shift that shapes a new way of experiencing, thinking, and relating emotionally to the plans of God. A divine collision with Jesus strips us of our religious rhetoric and hypocrisy and leaves us bowing in humility with a heart awakened to the identity of the King.

Compassionate Breakdown

Every old story has a breaking point; in Saul's case, it was Jesus' answer to his question: "I am Jesus whom you are persecuting." Here was Jesus, the head of the church, dealing with its chief antagonist, who would only be stopped by conversion or by death.

When Saul stood up, Jesus was gone and he was blind, so his friends took him by the hand and led him like a child to Damascus, where his entrance was far from what he'd planned. Instead of the triumphant Jewish crusader coming to imprison the followers of Jesus, he stumbled under escort through the gate.

Saul remained in a state of spiritual shock for three days, not eating or drinking. On the road he had literally been stopped in his tracks and physically knocked to the ground. His lifelong old story of religious perfection was coming apart. All he had believed was breaking down. Throughout those days in Damascus he was coming to grips with who Jesus was, along with the content and demands of His gospel of the kingdom. How would Saul respond? What would this mean for his life?

Yet, in time hope replaced despair in the breakdown, because Jesus showed Saul that a man named Ananias would come and lay hands on him that he might regain his sight. When Ananias arrived at the door, there was Saul, blind, gaunt from lack of nourishment, and in a state of confusion. Ananias spoke to Saul with incredible grace: "Brother Saul, the Lord Jesus . . . has sent me." Immediately there fell from Saul's eyes something like scales and he regained his sight.

But that was only one aspect of a breakdown happening in Saul on multiple levels. His disregard for Jesus now transformed into a living experience with the resurrected

Messiah. His hostile prejudice toward Christians was gone, the people he had sought to destroy now becoming channels of compassion and healing. From this point on he would heed a new calling to live for Jesus and to advance the growth of His church. This breakdown was so dramatic that Saul would carry it with him throughout his ministry, even after he became known as the apostle Paul.

This young radical zealot would eventually emerge to be used to take the message of Jesus and His kingdom to the unbelieving world. In fact, within days of his conversion, Saul launched into his new career, confounding the Jews who lived in Damascus by proving that Jesus is the Christ.

When your story collides with Jesus, expect long-held beliefs and practices to change. In the presence of Jesus nothing can remain the same. The contrast between our old story and Jesus is so great that it leads us to reorient our whole way of living. The breakdown is the beginning of something great.

Creative Breakthrough

Paul's breakthrough consisted of more than emotion. Another component provided form, structure, and content, giving incredible insight to serve him for all the years of his ministry: He experienced a breakthrough in his reading and understanding of the Scriptures. Paul had begun to reread the Old Testament and rethink its meaning. As a religious perfectionist, he had prided himself on his knowledge of the Word, but he was now beginning to *comprehend* the Scriptures, which have been written to instruct all of Jesus' followers (see 1 Corinthians 10:11). After his encounter with the risen Messiah, he could see that the Scriptures had been pointing toward Jesus all along. As Paul's relationship to God changed, his relationship to Scripture changed.

For the first time, Saul was able to see the depth and meaning he had overlooked as a pre-Christian Jew. Christ had transformed everything for him. All the Old Testament stories took on new meaning. When reading the story of Moses placing the veil over his face, Paul now saw a contrast between law and grace. Man's access to God was once limited to a select few, but Jesus had torn down that veil between God and man so the wonders of God could be experienced directly by many.

Paul's breakthrough also recast his understanding of prophecy concerning Jesus. His view of people was no longer defined by race, but according to the Spirit. In many cases the new meaning was not found in the text itself, but as a gift from the illuminating, revealing Spirit of God. Now the Old Testament functioned as a servant to the gospel of Jesus, to be read in light of Jesus.

In the past, Paul boasted mental mastery of the sacred text; now he was filled with a heart of submission.

This same attitude of submission is important for your Bible reading—especially for your discovery of your life verse. If we try to read our desired meaning into Scripture—to become its master—we will find ourselves misled. We must welcome and follow the guidance of the Spirit, reading the whole Bible in light of Jesus and His work.

The old saying is still true: Each passage of Scripture has one interpretation and many applications. The God who gave us the Bible still gives today, helping us understand the author's original intent (interpretation) along with the ways to live it in our time (application), eventually leading to inspiration.

Clear Beginning

Paul's revitalized reading of the Scripture text defined the way he saw himself and the call of God on his life. His task was to lay a foundation for the church and to make the Word fully known. His reading of the Old Testament would resonate in all his teaching, be it the breathtaking panorama of Romans or the personal letters to Timothy. Paul was still a man, well aware of his frailties and weaknesses, frank and open, never trying to hide his struggles behind his call. He learned that Jesus makes good use of weak people.

Parts of the Old Testament played an especially personal role in Paul's life. For him, the Scriptures were not just a source for his writings and sermons. Paul considered these ancient texts to be vitally relevant, *active* words that brought about change within him. He repeatedly applied them to his personal choices, as well as in his calling and ministry. He would say of his own preaching that, like Jeremiah, he was a man under compulsion. And he would emulate Moses in many aspects of his prophetic ministry.

Did Paul have a life verse? If I were going to guess at it, I'd say Habakkuk 2:4: "The righteous will live by his faith," or, as Paul would come to clarify it, "the justified one will live by faith."

As a lifelong Pharisee, Paul's focus had been on strict obedience to the law as the way of justifying his standing before God. But this religious approach turned out to be a death sentence. Paul came to realize that his pedigree was a dead end as a means to bringing about transformation, so with fresh eyes he read Habakkuk's prophecy. Paul had discovered that a life that pleases God is a life of faith, a life that treasures the promise of God, hears the Word with spiritual ears, and presses through difficult times in reliance on God.

Habakkuk 2:4 was more than a tagline for Paul; I'm convinced this was his life verse. He quoted it twice in places of prominence, each time with a different emphasis, like a newly minted coin held up to the light with each turn revealing a different glittering face. In Romans 1:17, Paul emphasized "the righteous man" (or "the justified one"), where he explained that he (and every Christian) was declared completely righteous in God's sight because of Jesus, not by keeping the law. In Galatians 3:11, "faith" was the focus. It was not the law nor Paul's self-will, but a living faith in Jesus that placed him in right standing.

This is one of the signs of a life verse—it never remains static but is renewed with each new season of life, with every new assignment taking on a fresh, new meaning.

Maybe you see yourself in Paul's journey. Maybe, like Saul, you've held back certain parts of your heart and refused to submit to God's Word, creating a disconnect between your knowledge and your heart. Reading the Bible to discover your life verse is an invitation to your own Damascus encounter. Prepare yourself for the healthiest collision of your life, resulting in freedom from all the hypocrisy and empty rhetoric, and fresh insight into the ancient paths of Scripture, leading to a living God.

You might begin by asking Paul's question: "Lord, who are You?" Then read Scripture, listening with an open heart to Jesus' reply to you.

Is Your Death Sentence Your Life Script?

Try a short exercise. See if you can distill your old story down into one sentence. Go ahead, try it. I'll wait.

Now, recite that sentence out loud.

You've just quoted your death sentence. That's what you're tempted to carry around with you and listen to every moment of every day. Do you wonder why you struggle?

Your death sentence *deceives with the truth*. A death sentence uses part of the truth to manufacture unworthiness and defeat, emphasizing the worst aspect of that truth. Maybe your parents didn't love you; so you assume that you're unlovable. Perhaps you were accepted only when you performed well; so you assume that your worth is based on your performance.

Many of us have had our death sentences reinforced by people who claimed to love us. It only takes a few choice words from a family member, a close friend, or a teacher. Maybe they spoke the words in passing or as a jest, but we cling to the words, keeping them lodged in our hearts. The death sentence becomes our truth.

Whatever the death sentence you've believed, it's wrong! You have more talent, more potential, and far more to offer this world—and to offer God—than that label. You have greater worth and are capable of far more than your death sentence. What God says about you and your destiny out-weighs any of the world's classifications.

Your death sentence *drives negative action*. A death sentence will always cause us to make wrong decisions. We have a way of attracting others to us who have similar death sentences, so if you want to know what you think about yourself, then look at the people you hang out with.

A death sentence makes us think every relationship comes with strings attached. It causes us to distrust others, to be suspicious of their motives, to hesitate in taking hold of great opportunities.

Our death sentence knocks our faith and assurance out from under us, so in a desperate search for security we run to everybody else, trying to get them to tell us who we are. We run to the clubs, the gym, the store, to work. We look everywhere to try to find significance and value.

Your death sentence *distorts divine motivation*. We often doubt that God would simply give us a particular blessing because He loves us, so we try to give God a reason to bless us. We make unnecessary deals with God, trying to buy His favor. *God, I'll get it together. I'll clean up my life. I'll try harder . . . just get me out of this, and I promise I'll never do it again!* But God offers His grace free of charge; anything we do is an expression of gratitude, not a swap for God's favor.

If your old story has its way, it will keep you from understanding that God loves you for who you *are*, not what you *do*.

Dismantling a death sentence requires an honest examination of life. Here are some questions to help you uncover the influence of a death sentence:

> *Do you go into situations expecting the worst?*
> *Do you go into opportunities with a chip on your shoulder?*
> *Do you scrutinize your relationships, looking for any possible slight or mistreatment?*
> *Do you wear people out with excessive questioning?*
> *Do you constantly compare yourself to others?*
> *Do you worry about how other people view you?*
> *Do you sabotage good relationships by being too hard on yourself?*

Ten Sure Ways to Live Your Death Sentence

Of course, no one purposefully chooses a death sentence as the goal of his or her life. But if you are stubbornly set on doing life your own way, then here are ten guaranteed ways to let your death sentence fulfill its full potential. If, on the other hand, you are ready to enjoy the abundant life that God has promised, then use this list to detect the presence and influence of a death sentence, so that you can replace it with God's new story:

1. Cut off ties from family and friends, so there is no one to encourage you, to give you understanding and living support.
2. Stop depending on God.
3. Always live in the past.
4. Become overly critical of yourself and judgmental of others.
5. Always demand that everything goes your way.

6. Stop laughing, refuse to enjoy life.
7. Hold on to your negative habits and pessimistic thinking.
8. Never ask for God's help.
9. Be unwilling to learn and grow.
10. Define your significance by what you do, and forget about who you really are.

Letting your death sentence lead your life will guarantee a life of hopelessness and needless suffering, while also creating a deep sense of unworthiness and a loss of self-control and energy.

Death Sentence or Life Verse?
A collision of stories happens when your death sentence runs into your life verse. Even though the two are very different, they have similarities. For example, both have innovative power—one to create, one to destroy. Whichever one we choose to believe will produce tangible results in life. But by choosing to believe a death sentence, we are more likely to live recklessly and to experience pain, suffering, alienation, and isolation. Choosing to believe your life verse opens you up to a life of peace, hope, and confidence.

Both produce their own internal dialogue in our thoughts: A death sentence fosters negative self-talk, which causes obstacles to living well, while the voice of a life verse is always one of positive expectancy, elevating our thinking and encouraging hope even in the most dire circumstance.

Both program us to go through life in a particular way.

Both impact our mental state and energy level. Both influence our relationships with others.

Every day, as we make choices under the influence of a death sentence or a life verse, one or the other forms a pattern that defines the perception of others about us, determining how others react to us.

A *death sentence* is made up of words chosen by human reasoning.

A *life verse* is an infallible statement spoken by God.

A *death sentence* limits the capacity of our lives.

A *life verse* lifts us up to live toward our full potential.

A *death sentence* lives in the past.

A *life verse* looks to the future.

A *death sentence* creates blame, shame, and guilt.

A *life verse* empowers authentic living.

A *death sentence* pulls back from opportunity.

A *life verse* leans forward into opportunity.

Which one has control in your life? Something is going to give your life its shape and direction. Something is going to determine what gives (or claims to give) your life ultimate value. One of the earliest places these two choices are presented in Scripture appears in Deuteronomy 30:19: "I have set before you life and death, the blessing and the curse. So choose life in order that you may live." You always have a choice as to what will shape your life.

Here are some questions to ask yourself in order to reveal what the old story has been telling you and, by extension, what a life verse can offer you.

> *How is my old story controlling my choices?*

> *What price am I paying?*

> *Do I believe there's a better way?*

> *How would doing things differently change what is happening to me?*

> *What are the costs and benefits of change?*

CHAPTER 4

Outgrow Your Story

GOD HAS MORE FOR YOU.

Doesn't reading that sentence stir something inside you? The hope that God intends your life to mean even more than you think it does now? Something's alive in you; the desire of your heart is reaching for something more.

Could it be that we've let our lives be limited by our thoughts? Does the following sentiment sound familiar: "I haven't lived as I should, so God cannot work in my life." Behind that thought is the assumption that we have to perform in certain ways to earn God's acceptance. That assumption is false. Such thinking makes our journey of faith about the limited bit we can do, rather than the immeasurable greatness of what God can do.

Let's be clear: The spiritual journey is not about thinking positively or developing a good self-image or even doing good things. It's not about trying to prove to God that we are worthy enough to be blessed. It is about coming before Him as we really are, not pretending or posturing in His presence, and waking up to the reality that we can't make ourselves right. It's about inviting *Him* to do *His* work in us.

I've spent the last twenty years speaking all over the country, and I get one question a lot: "Hey, do you remember me?" Sometimes I do remember; sometimes I don't. When I don't, I feel put on the spot. I want to save both myself and the questioner from embarrassment, so I've developed few generic responses to the question—responses that usually help me bluff my way through the conversation.

But none of us can get away for long with faking a deep personal love of God and His Word. We might fool some people (including ourselves) with vague generalities and catch phrases like "Well, you know the Good Book says . . ." or "I love all the Bible's stories." But many of the big statements people make about the Bible are meant to mask a lack of personal connection. In this chapter we will take time to remove the awkwardness of having to pretend.

We all pick and choose what we let others see about us. We do the same thing with God, trying to show Him we are lovable through our behavior. The problem with this is that it requires neither repentance nor brokenness. It avoids that necessary change in our thinking that shifts the focus from us to Jesus. We like to feel good and avoid pain, but the truth is, no matter how much you hurt, no matter how miserable your old story has made you, without an intentional decision to let your pain take you to a new place, nothing new will happen.

God has more for you.

But don't take my word for it. The words of the first epistle of John help to guide toward a life-word experience.

Outgrown the Old

That which was from the beginning, which we have heard, which we have seen with our eyes, which we have looked at and our hands have touched—this we proclaim concerning the Word of life. The life appeared; we have seen it and testify to it, and we proclaim to you the eternal life, which was with the Father and has appeared to us. (1 John 1:1-2, NIV)

John, whose words you just read, was one of the youngest of Jesus' disciples, and he lived into old age—the last survivor of the Twelve. He lived to see an astounding variety of lies perpetrated in the name of Jesus Christ—strange mixes of Christianity with other world religions, some denying the incarnation of Christ, some denying His resurrection. He heard countless voices trying to win people over. And in the midst of this confusion, above all the false voices, John cried out, "I've seen Him, heard Him, touched Him. You can take my word for it. Take the Word of Life!"

John had grown up with his own version of the old story—one in which religion was a matter of external prac-tices: reading Torah, going to temple, obeying the Law, and observing the feast. Everything was about right behavior. Meeting Jesus changed all that for John. All those years spent traveling with Jesus awakened his soul. John knew the true gospel because he was there when it began. He had been a friend of the Word of Life. And as Jesus led John deeper into his new story, John found himself outgrowing the old.

Can you remember a time when you outgrew your pants? Okay, stay with me and keep in mind: Pain is good. Remember, the waist got tighter and started to cut into your skin. You finally faced the reality that you couldn't breathe. You needed new pants that would fit because the old pair simply was not working anymore.

Just as with those pants, there comes a time when you start to outgrow your old story, because it doesn't fit who you are anymore. The only way to remove the pain is to remove the restricting story and replace it with one that fits better. It's through this hope that we find a better strategy for thinking about ourselves, and therefore for living.

There are five steps to outgrowing your story:

> *Decide on a new perspective.*
> *Depend on your new partnership.*
> *Discover the plotline.*
> *Disarm the power.*
> *Don't pick on yourself.*

Decide on a New Perspective

Do not be conformed to this world, but be transformed by the renewing of your mind. (Romans 12:2)

The old story has been playing without our even being aware of it. Like Muzak in an elevator, you can block it out of consciousness, but it's still playing, and in the right situations it can drive you nuts. As our first step, we have to decide that it's time to put on our grown-up pants and get our thinking straight. Without the decision to change, we will stay stuck in the same patterns, held by the same pain.

I've met many people who have lots of money, great jobs, and good families, but are miserable because they have not outgrown their old stories. It's a simple but powerful truth: If you want to change your life, you have to change your mind.

So we must decide to make the effort to uncover our old stories and get free of the rules they have placed on us. We stop letting the old story live through us, then God's story can take hold, in part as we discover our life verse.

Depend on Your New Partnership

What we have seen and heard we proclaim to you
also, so that you too may have fellowship with us;
and indeed our fellowship is with the Father, and
with His Son Jesus Christ. (1 John 1:3)

John pointed out that this life is not an exercise in academia but a relationship. He wanted his readers to take hold of a fellowship, a relationship with the Father and the Son. Believing the Word of Life brings us into a friendship, a family. This is the relationship John had experienced, and every believer can enjoy this same fellowship.

Fellowship means to be intimately bound, a perfect description of the believer's relationship to Jesus. It means to participate in partnership. We have fellowship with God because we know Christ. We have fellowship because we have received the truth.

How do we find a new story? By plugging into the power in partnership with Jesus. When we live off in some other story without Jesus, we are as powerless as an unplugged toaster. Jesus invites us to participate in the kind of life He lived.

The task of getting out of old stories can seem to be too much, and sometimes it feels like it would just be easier to manage the old one by trying to get along. But remember:

God has more for you.

And we are not in this journey alone. Jesus, through His death and resurrection, disarmed everything that could keep us from the life we are to live. The past event of the Cross was never meant to stay in the past—rather His saving work is to be experienced in our present lives. In the past, Christ has worked through the Cross, which means He is the source of new life. But we must not miss that He is also working in the present to give us the ability to be our real selves. Jesus' present ministry inside us is our hope for finding a new story.

Discover the Plotline

This is the message we have heard from Him and announce to you, that God is Light, and in Him there is no darkness at all. If we say that we have fellowship with Him and yet walk in the darkness, we lie and do not practice the truth. (1 John 1:5-6)

Discovery of a new story begins by understanding the influence of yesterday. You have lived the life you've lived so far and that's a fact. There is a moment when you stop and listen and discover that the plotline you've been living doesn't have to continue on. You no longer have to be controlled by the past. Stopping and listening raises our awareness that we have a choice.

Are you aware of your old story? I know of a pastor who, when preparing for a sermon series, asked some of his members what were the reoccurring struggles in their lives. Here are a few of their responses:

> *"As soon as I achieve significant weight loss, I put it all back on."*
> *"Every time I advance in my career, I do something to blow it."*
> *"Whenever I get into a great relationship, I wind up ruining it."*

Living in unwanted and unhealthy stories is more frustrating than anything else. But once you are alert, aware, and ready to get out of those old plotlines, you're one step closer to launching your new story and finding your life verse. Once you bring the old story into the light, it will begin to lose its power.

We will do almost anything to avoid confronting our old story—shop, eat, drink, lie, run away. Instead of letting the story create these avoidance actions, stop and sit with it. What has it been telling you? Most people don't want to slow down enough to listen to their story and find out how they've contributed to their own hurt. Stopping and listening means we turn off the autopilot.

By stopping and listening to the old story, we interrupt its message and find that we have a fighting chance. If a smoke alarm goes off, it's an indication there's fire nearby. If you are ready to listen to the old story, then you'll have to think about what you're thinking about. Where do you feel hurt, angry, ashamed, or abandoned? Where are those hurts present?

Give them conscious attention; don't leave the unconscious patterns in charge.

Disarm the Old Power

If we walk in the Light as He Himself is in the Light,
we have fellowship with one another, and the blood
of Jesus His Son cleanses us from all sin. (1 John 1:7)

Things happen to us that are beyond our control. We feel like victims, and for some these experiences and circumstances become their story. But playing the perpetual victim means there's no way out of the old story. Here's the good news: That powerlessness no longer describes you! Really! It's a relic of the past.

How then do we walk away from these stories? As we bring our story into the light, we bring the Word of Life into our story. If there is ever going to be a change in perspective, we have to get God into our story.

See if these old story lines sound familiar:

Listen to Your Old Story	Look at God's Word	Live a New Story
"People love me then leave me."	[God] Himself has said, "I will never desert you, nor will I ever forsake you." (Hebrews 13:5)	"God will help me risk letting people get close. Even if people fail me, God won't."
"People don't get me."	The LORD . . . will exult over you with joy, He will be quiet in His love, He will rejoice over you with shouts of joy. (Zephaniah 3:17)	"I have shortcomings, and some criticisms of me are justified. God accepts me with my strengths and weaknesses, and so will I."
"In order to be loved, I can't be me."	I am convinced that [nothing] will be able to separate us from the love of God. (Romans 8:38-39)	"God loves me as I am. Therefore I am lovable. I'll find the people who will love me for who I am.
"I have to look a certain way in order to be loved."	I will give thanks to You, for I am fearfully and wonderfully made. (Psalm 139:14)	"Inner character will make me attractive to the right kinds of people."
"It's everybody else's fault."	As for me, I shall walk in my integrity. (Psalm 26:11)	"God will give me insight and courage to take responsibility for my own faults and to forgive when I'm not at fault."

Each truth we download into our lives must be rehearsed, practiced, repeated in our heads and hearts. Eventually the Word becomes the lens by which we interpret the events of life. Taking God's Word over the words of others—even over our own—is the first step of disarming the death sentences we've lived under. Getting God's eternal words—especially your life verse—into everyday life changes our thinking.

Walking away from your story means shifting your perspective; because of Christ we have a choice over what happens next. We no longer have to play these roles; the old stories are not our future. Discovering your life verse switches your perspective by putting Jesus in the picture, allowing you to see your old story for the fabrication it is, while simultaneously moving on from it.

Don't Pick on Yourself

If we confess our sins, He is faithful and righteous to forgive us our sins and to cleanse us from all unrighteousness. (1 John 1:9)

Facing hard truths about ourselves is never easy, and often we respond by turning the blame on ourselves, judging ourselves harshly. Stepping away from your story is not an exercise in condemnation. It's not about calling yourself weak or needy or a failure, because judging yourself without mercy just covers the truth and delays change. There is a better way.

He [became] a merciful and faithful high priest . . . because he himself suffered. (Hebrews 2:17-18, NIV)

There's nothing harder to deal with than a deep sense of failure. Our minds flood with remorse and cripple us at the very point where we need power. But Jesus is our sympathetic High Priest; through His word and work, the sins of our old story are forgiven, and the guilt connected to our old roles is taken away. The past can no longer keep us from finding our new story.

Jesus did not live a life detached from adversity and

trouble; He experienced these firsthand. The hazards, the hardships—He experienced them all for us. He feels for us, and He's sympathetic because He's been through this life.

Jesus lived our stories.

All the forces of evil were hurled against Him on the cross, but He overcame! He is fully able to bring you out of your old story and into a new one. Knowing that He's the sympathetic High Priest leads us to forgiveness.

You don't need to judge yourself; Christ was judged for you. He dealt with the situation already; He did what was necessary to give you a new story.

But don't take my word for it.

For by one sacrifice he has made perfect forever those who are being made holy. (Hebrews 10:14, NIV)

See? God has more for you.

In the next chapter we continue this journey in discovery of your life verse. Before we talk about what a life verse *is*, it is important to know what a life verse *is not*.

PART II

WELL-VERSED: THE WORLD OF THE LIFE VERSE

I GREW UP in the town of Aizu Wakamatsu. It's a castle town—home of one of the oldest samurai castles in Japan. The people of my city are honest, steady, and persevering. These characteristics have been handed down for many generations.

My earliest memory of discovering my life verse was when I was eight or nine years old. Every day I would walk to school, and on my way I would pass a Catholic church. The street in front of the church had power poles that lined each side of the street, and on the poles hung the most beautiful banners in every color. To my eight-year-old eyes it looked like they lined the street for miles. The banners were eight feet tall and six feet wide, pulled tight by the breeze. On the banners were printed sayings or phrases. At first I wasn't sure if they were quotes; I didn't know where they were from. But every day I read those banners and memorized the words of each one.

I found out they were verses from the Bible. I told my mom I wanted to learn the Bible, so she had one of the nuns from the church come to my house each day to teach me about the Bible. The nun showed me how to find each of those verses I had been reading on those beautiful banners. I looked up every verse I had seen. I remember reading Philippians 4:4: "Rejoice in the Lord always; again I will say, rejoice!"

That verse became my verse. When I read it I felt the peace of God; I felt like my heart was being held by His heart. From that day on, no matter what happened to me, my heart answered my situations with "Rejoice!" I could always hear the words of that verse in my head and heart. That verse comforted me in school, in the workplace, and in my personal life.

That was many years ago. I've since been married and become the mother of two boys, whom I love very much. My boys have brought me much rejoicing. To this day I feel the assurance of God through that verse.

—KYOKO

It was a few years ago that I met Kyoko. Her younger son, Alex, was the victim of a break-in; he had been brutally murdered, shot execution style in the back of the head. The perpetrator had violated house arrest multiple times. The police caught and arrested the murderer. Then there was Alex's funeral, a vigil of all of Alex's friends, followed by hearings, trials, postponements. As the legal system plodded on its slow path to justice, Kyoko sat through multiple hearings, TV interviews, newspaper articles. She had to relive the last hours of Alex's life many times over. She pressed on through it all. I'm amazed at her courage and her warm smile to others.

I asked her if she was ever angry at the guilty party, the system, or God. Did she ever shake her fist at God?

"No, never," she said.

"How have you managed this ordeal?"

She looked at me and said, "Rejoice in the Lord always; again I will say, rejoice!"

✦   ✦   ✦

God's Word changes us. Please visit YourLifeVerse.org and let us know your life verse and how it has changed your life.

CHAPTER 5

What Your Life Verse Is Not

LET'S TAKE a brief look at some passages of Scripture that will probably *not* be your life verse. Or anyone's, really . . .

Jeremiah 19:9, ESV: "And I will make them eat the flesh of their sons and their daughters, and everyone shall eat the flesh of his neighbor." (It is not nice to eat your neighbors.)

First Corinthians 7:29, NIV: "What I mean, brothers and sisters, is that the time is short. From now on those who have wives should live as if they do not." (The NFL enthusiast's life verse.)

Ezekiel 4:15, KJV: "I have given thee cow's dung for man's dung, and thou shalt prepare thy bread therewith." (No comment.)

Leviticus 19:19, NIV: "Do not wear clothing woven of two kinds of material." (Cotton/polyester blends forbidden.)

Ecclesiastes 2:17, NLT: "Everything is meaningless." (Life verse for the days you spend in airports.)

Deuteronomy 2:3, NIV: "You have made your way around this hill country long enough; now turn north." (A word of encouragement if you ever break down in West Memphis, Arkansas.)

Joshua 9:12, NIV: "This bread of ours was warm when . . . we left. . . . But now see how dry and moldy it is." (If this is your verse, you probably live with four other dudes in a house you rent a mile from campus, and you should trick one of your girlfriends into cleaning your kitchen.)

Finding your life verse is easy—if you know what you're looking for. So why haven't more people discovered their own life verses?

With most forms of reading we are bystanders, onlookers of the content. The tendency in reading Scripture is to place ourselves over the text, making ourselves the final judge of the usefulness of the content and what we will do with what we read. However, in reading for a life verse, we become *participants*. The way the Bible is composed is meant to draw us in. Reading Scripture is not just concerned with learning facts, so if our only pursuit in reading Scripture is information, we miss the depth and texture.

Reading the Bible is not like reading other books, so in order to find your life verse and use it correctly, it's helpful to know what your life verse is *not*. Here are eleven things a life verse is not.

It's Not a Sound Bite

Our culture has developed the amazing ability to distill stories into a single sentence. Whether on billboards, the front pages of tabloids, or talk shows, the sound bite has become the way we receive our information. These fragments of information floating through digital space become so definitive that it's no wonder we have trouble reading the Bible.

Discovering your life verse is not a matter of skimming the headlines the way we do while standing in the checkout line at the supermarket. Reading Scripture means allowing yourself to be brought into the large, real world of God's story. Sentence by sentence, we are led into a story that makes our story new and eternally meaningful.

It's Not a Motto or a Slogan

Most of us have a handy arsenal of clever phrases that we say to ourselves when things get difficult. "Everything happens for a reason." "When the going gets tough, the tough get going." Handy, maybe, but definitely not scriptural.

To use Scripture in this manner is to flatten the richness of its eternal truth.

Typically a slogan is a catchy saying used by a politician to make himself or herself more recognizable. Sometimes it's a phrase used by a company to get you to believe in their product, so you'll feel good when you and your money part ways at the time of purchase. Other times it's used as a catchphrase, like when someone tells a long story that seems to have no point and then says, "But I saved 15 percent on my car insurance."

The words of God were never meant to be used as a tagline. There is far too much content tucked away in those verses.

It's Not a Brand

When you think of a brand, you might think of a swoosh mark, a piece of fruit, or a particular automobile emblem. It's an image that's used to associate visually with the product itself. But the words of God are not separate from God; they are God-breathed words as powerful as those He used to create existence.

Genesis loudly proclaims, "God said." God spoke and it came into being. This is the premise of Scripture. The Word and life are the same thing. Life begins with the Word and the Word makes life. We find this truth living in the pages of Scripture. Our life is brought into contact with the words of God, and we discover that there are no words that God does not intend for us to live out.

In the world of Christian knickknacks, you might find a plaque, a key ring, or a greeting card with your name on it with a verse written below it. When done in a way that trivializes Scripture, this might be cute, but it minimizes the power of God's Word. Sometimes Christians will print a verse on their business cards or checks. Many times famous Christians will scribble a verse next to their autograph. That's fine, unless it's just a little extra something that makes a signature look cooler.

The life verse God has for you is far more than a little reference next to your name. It's more than a neat way to make your business more spiritual. Your life verse was never meant to function as an accessory or as a way to call attention to yourself. Your personal verse is to make God's presence obvious by living out the Word through your life.

It's Not a Fortune Cookie

We've all had the experience of eating Chinese food and walking away completely stuffed, only to be hungry again twenty minutes later. (Which, by the way, is how you feel when you read Scripture just for surface information, not for life change.) Usually at the end of the meal it's customary to receive a fortune cookie. Inside is a piece of paper printed with a saying that is usually so vague it could apply to anyone, anywhere. On the other side of the paper are a set of "lucky numbers," which I always like to punch into my phone to see whom fortune will connect me to.

It's easy to treat Scripture like a series of these fortune-cookie sayings. It's understandable that people might see it that way—just looking at a page of the Bible gives that impression. With all the numbered chapters and verses, it can look like a lengthy catalog of stand-alone texts that can be chosen randomly and combined haphazardly to determine our destiny.

But the Scriptures are God communicating Himself to real people in the context of real life. That's why so much of the Bible is written as stories—true, historic stories. Within those pages is a God who lives in a close, personal relationship with His people. When it comes to reading the Word of God, context is everything, so reading whole chapters and books is important. Finding your life verse happens when you read Scripture in the context in which it was written, because no text can be accurately understood out of context.

It takes the whole Bible to give understanding to any part of the Bible.

We already know this instinctively; even our daily conversation has context. When we speak to our friends or kids, the sentences of our lives are not spoken in isolation. The same is true with our life verses.

It's Not a Mission Statement

A mission statement is related to a work, a task, or an assignment for an individual or a group and is usually a set of propositions about the purpose of an organization.

This is not a life verse.

A life verse does not orbit around your work. Your work might be influenced by your life verse, but not the other way around. The temptation for us all is to define ourselves by what we do and the roles we play, instead of by who God says we are. Your life verse encompasses *everything* that is in your life and yet is more than that, serving as an overarching theme. This does not mean your specific verse won't contain instructions that directly impact your work and your roles in life, but think of your life verse as a frame that goes around your past, present, and future.

It's Not a Promise

This may seem shocking at first. While I was speaking at a conference, I mentioned I was writing a book on life verses. One of the attendees spoke up. "I have a whole box of promises." She reached into her bag and pulled out a small blue box filled with index cards, each containing a promise, all filed under various topics. There are eight hundred promises in the Scriptures, certainly more than enough for all the circumstances we face.

A life verse may *contain* a promise within it, but it is so much bigger than just a promise. A life verse is a statement that includes your whole life, that shapes the vision for your life. A life verse does more than merely guide your actions; it shows you who you are.

It's Not for You and Your Spouse

It's yours. There *is* a verse for your marriage, but that's a different assignment for another time. Your life verse is yours—it's something God has spoken to you about your life as an individual.

Each of us carries his or her life verse into marriage, and without question, discovering your unique identity as a child of God directly impacts your role as a husband or a wife. If you are married and don't know your life verse, then each of you should use the path laid out in this book to find it. Your way of thinking about your relationship with your spouse will be changed for the better. If you are single, then this is the perfect season for you. Every word of God has shaping power, and God's verse for you will help you in learning how to build any successful relationship.

It's Not Something You Pick

God gives your life verse to you through the work of the Holy Spirit as you read His Word. *Your life verse will find you.*

Pulling up a group of verses by topic, then scrolling through the list until you find one you like, is just playing Bible roulette. That is not the same thing as discovering it by having God reveal it to you while you read His Word.

The journey through the Word is as important as the destination: finding your life verse.

It's Not a Quick Fix

A life verse is not magic; life doesn't fall into place because you've found a verse. You still have struggles, the demands of everyday living, and always the pressure of circumstances. We are always tempted to reach for a quick fix to patch up a problem that's ruptured. There is the danger of using Scripture to sentimentalize life, or using Scripture to escape the realities of life. Scripture was never designed to be used as a bandage for problems that actually need surgery. However, having a life verse gives you a faith-based focus, an awareness that in the midst of life's grind God is at work. A life verse calls our attention to the truth that in the course of life's difficulties, God is revealing Himself. It gives us courage and insight to face and handle life God's way. We are in fact participants with God and His Word; your life verse is meant to be lived. Your verse is there as a constant reminder that whether times are tough or easy, good or bad, there's meaning.

It's Not About You

That sounds counterintuitive, I know. After all, discovering a life verse specially designed for you is the whole point of this book. But here's my point: The purpose of your life verse is not to make you feel better about you—it's to reveal and point you to Jesus. The story line of the Bible goes like this: God creates man and woman . . . we break relationship with God . . . God pursues us to win us back to Himself . . . God's rescue mission succeeds in Jesus. All of Scripture is about Jesus—how He came to live, die, and rise again. This includes the Old Testament as well. After Jesus' resurrection, He appeared to the disciples and showed how He was foretold and revealed in the Old Testament:

> These are My words which I spoke to you while I was still with you, that all things which are written about Me in the Law of Moses and the Prophets and the Psalms must be fulfilled. (Luke 24:44)

The phrase, "the Law . . . the Prophets and the Psalms," is inclusive of the entire Old Testament. The whole Old Testament is about Jesus, not just a few verses. No matter where you are reading in Scripture, it's wise to ask how Jesus can be seen there. The whole Bible anticipated Jesus' coming, suffering, and resurrection. Jesus is the point of Scripture.

And Jesus is the point of your life verse. As we will see throughout this book, as that verse works its way into your life, it will help keep you aware of the presence of Jesus.

It's Not a Gimmick

Psalm 1 presents contrasting pictures that illustrate the real way a life verse can help transform an old story into a new story.

How blessed is the man who does not walk in the counsel of the wicked, nor stand in the path of sinners, nor sit in the seat of scoffers! (verse 1)

Your old story came from bad counsel; from the examples of people who followed a destructive path; from destructive attitudes. But see what a difference a new story makes:

But his delight is in the law of the LORD, and in His law he meditates day and night. (verse 2)

The source of the new story is the Word of God. ("The law" here means the written Word of God.) And I would urge you to read and learn widely from throughout the whole Bible, which will provide context and fuller meaning for your life verse. This source is reliable, solid ground for spiritual growth; the way of the old story is vague, swampy, based on subjective experience. Your new story will be defined in part when you find your life verse in God's Word.

We are to live in response to our life verse rather than in the counsel and path of the wicked. This is the challenge: to step away from your old story and toward the new, including finding your life verse and meditating on it frequently. ("Meditating" simply means thinking it over, working it into the fiber of your being.) Let your life verse so saturate your life that it takes the place of your old story. This helps anchor your new story in place of the old.

He will be like a tree firmly planted by streams of water, which yields its fruit in its season . . . and in whatever he does, he prospers. (verse 3)

Just as the roots of that tree are firmly planted in a source that nourishes and produces fruit, so it is with us spiritually. The source we draw from? God's written Word, with your life verse feeding the central taproot. Your life verse is eternal and will produce in you a solidly grounded new story. You'll become like a tree with roots penetrating deep into the very heart of God, strong enough to withstand whatever comes your way.

Long Ago, on a Seashore Far, Far Away
Hopefully this chapter has removed some of the false assumptions about life verses.

Now prepare yourself for a journey more than three thousand years into the past. God's people stand on the edge of a new day, on the edge of the Red Sea. This is the moment for which Israel has waited all these long centuries. Egypt lies behind, the Promised Land lies ahead.

They're about to live their life verse . . .

CHAPTER 6

The Power of
Your Life Verse

WHO DOESN'T love a good story? Whether it's a movie, an episodic TV show, a Broadway play, a good book, or watching someone injure himself on YouTube, a story has power. It's memorable, and if really good, it's always worth retelling or retweeting. That is, unless the storyteller can't tell it well.

There are many ways to make a good story go bad. Here are some good examples of story killers:

"You Had to Be There"
We've all been around a person who tells a story in great detail, with a complete setup that creates anticipation . . . only to end without a point, followed by an awkward pause, then punctuated with, "Well, I guess you had to be there." I guess not. It sounds like I would've hated being there.

"You Do the Math"

This person's story contains only fuzzy details, like, "So I was downtown and I had to be uptown and, so, well . . . you do the math." I would do the math if your story contained any numbers.

"Like I Said"

A "like I said" story happens when someone tells a story using that phrase authoritatively. The only problem is that they haven't said what they say they've said. Most of the time, "like I said" is followed by a quote that, up to that point in the story, hasn't actually been said.

"To Make a Long Story Short"

This can be irritating, because most of the time when this phrase appears in a story, it leaves out important details that would have given the story real impact. For instance, "So I was grocery shopping . . . well, to make a long story short, I just got out of prison." Hmm . . . I think you could've made that story a little longer.

Checking the Details

Couples are notorious for this genre of story. It begins with a simple premise, like driving to the mall, but becomes mired in minute details that don't improve the story. The husband starts: "So we drove to the mall," then turns to his wife and says, "Was it Tuesday or Wednesday?"

"Oh, I think it was Tuesday," she says, "because that was the day I was on the phone with—"

"Right, okay," he continues, "so when we were driving, we were on Britton road . . . wait . . ." He turns to his wife. "Was it Britton or Nichols?" Then he continues without letting her answer. "I forget," he says, "sometimes we take May Avenue. Well, anyway that evening—or was it afternoon? Well, I don't remember . . ."

By this time I'm weary of all their endless, irrelevant fact-checking. I don't want to hear about their trip; I want to interrupt: "So, to make a long story short . . ."

"Having Said That"

This phrase has recently gained popularity. "Having said that" is the new passive-aggressive way of saying you really don't like something or someone. It goes like this: "I think he is really talented and a great worker. Having said that, he's basically a jerk."

A Well-Versed Life

Another strategy for poor storytelling is getting lost in the trees and failing to see the forest. Many times in our lives, the whole of our story gets blurred so that we see only the bits and the pieces, the fragments instead of the complete picture.

Israel had a story—one in which they were both the storytellers and the listeners. Israel's original story included silence from God. A lot of it. A sense of absence, the feeling that God had abandoned them. His apparent apathy led to confusion. The plotlines of Israel's story were unresolved. They were living a death sentence.

But a shift in the story was about to take place—one that

would bring clarity and coherence to every part and detail. Israel's Exodus became the defining story of their identity, their destiny, their relationship with God, their freedom.

The book of Exodus began with the Israelites at the lowest point of their story. They were in Egypt, churning out bricks for Pharaoh's elaborate building projects. Egypt was the little nation's old story—really the only story Israel knew. They'd existed in this sad state for hundreds of years. Gone were the days of the national hero, Joseph, along with the promises once made to the legendary patriarchs—Abraham, Isaac, and Jacob. Egypt was ruled by a Pharaoh who believed he was a god, and the land with its majesty and beauty made his claim even more believable. Israel was on the losing side; all the odds were against them.

But God was at work, rewriting Israel's story. He hadn't forgotten them after all.

Moses, God's representative, through a series of confrontations and plagues, exposed the old story that was Egypt and revealed the possibility of a new story for Israel. Finally, Pharaoh had had enough and gladly set them free. Until he realized he was losing his low-cost labor. He changed his mind, took an army of six hundred horses and chariots, and went after them.

Pharaoh caught up to where Israel was camped by the Red Sea, and Israel knew they were trapped—the sea in front of them and Pharaoh closing in behind them. They had no way out. Israel's old story was *literally* about to overtake them once again.

Then, Moses spoke: "The Egyptians whom you have seen

today, you will never see them again" (Exodus 14:13). Moses stretched his staff over the sea and the waters parted. Israel walked through on dry land. The Egyptians continued in fierce pursuit. Until the waters poured back over them. In a moment, the power of the old story was ended by the greater power. A new story was beginning.

The Exodus story became Israel's life verse. The beginning of Israel's faith and confidence, it formed the sweeping story line of Israel's life, to be told and retold to future generations. It formed their confessions of God. They remembered (and still remember) it with an annual meal; they sang it as their song. Israel's new story was so powerful to their spiritual formation that it's repeated fifty times throughout Scripture.

What is true for Israel is true for us—once we were held captive by an old story, but God stepped into our lives on our behalf and did what we could never do for ourselves: He gave us a new story.

The new story is not fantasy. God doesn't make believe that suddenly everything is better. But where the old story isolated us from hope, God's new story begins with God Himself personally entering into life with all its imperfections, difficulties, struggles, and disappointments. Then He goes to work, patiently making the broken whole, helping the hurting, and forgiving, loving, and changing life according to the new story.

Israel's new story recast their experiences with God in fresh words. As life moved forward, a new generation was born after the Red Sea rescue—a generation who had not witnessed the Exodus or the parting of the waters. An entire book of the Bible, Deuteronomy, was written to help the children of Israel remember what God had done and to help them discover the power of their life verse. Moses directed the parents of the next generation of Israel to tell the story of God's redeeming work, His deliverance, His leadership. He wanted the students to see that the faith of Israel was the result of God's dynamic work in their actual history, not merely abstract ideas.

Like the Exodus story, your life verse becomes a lens through which all of life is viewed, reminding you of intervention and guidance as the real work of God. God is at the center of our life verses, the focal point. He is more powerful than the limitations of our old stories; He empathizes with the helpless and suffering and responds with action on behalf of the powerless. Throughout the remainder of this chapter we will examine several ways your life verse will serve you, as illustrated by the Exodus and the ways this new story shaped the Israelites.

Puts Life in Context

We were slaves to Pharaoh in Egypt, and the
LORD brought us from Egypt with a mighty hand.
(Deuteronomy 6:21)

From that unexpected moment when Israel was radically altered, they understood life differently. "We were slaves and now we are free." The sweeping events of Israel's deliverance were recounted over and over, retold from one generation to the next. Israel's experience is summarized succinctly in the nation's life verse, and they found countless ways to retell the story down through the ages. This way they would never forget the source of their freedom; they would always know what to expect from God in the future. Israel's life verse has stood the test of reason and the wear and tear of time. The Exodus formed the context through which they viewed life, and we read other instances in the Bible where the Exodus is used to interpret later events in Israel's history: The crossing of the Jordan was seen as another exodus, and during the Babylonian exile the prophet Isaiah announced the future return of Israel to their land by way of a new exodus.

In a number of ways a life verse puts life in proper context and helps us interpret life.

A life verse *is always broad enough to include all of life.* Israel is not reciting dreams or impressions, but rather facts, realities, points of time that can be identified, circumstances that can be defined. They did not make up history or modify it in the retelling; they literally lived in the new story.

A life verse *always takes the facts into account.* For Israel, "we were slaves" was the starting place of their story, and the same is true for us. Our journey to a new story starts with this: We were in darkness, and no human strength delivered us—God stretched out His arm and brought us out. We too had a Deliverer, just as Israel had; He died for the unjust that He might bring us to God. The actions and words of God reveal His concern and purpose for His people. The distinctiveness of a life verse is that it summarizes your entire life. With your life verse as the background of your life, nothing is without purpose.

A life verse *is personal.* It's not meant to be an abstract idea. God's great rescue of Israel changed them; when they quoted their life verse, they were recounting what God had done for them. If they were just reciting somebody else's circumstances, events, and anecdotes, the story would be impersonal and empty. Our lives will be connected to the life verses God has given us. You can quote random verses all day long, and who cares? But personalize it and show how it bears upon your life, and you'll recognize yourself living out your life verse.

A life verse *forms character.* The result of living in response to your life verse is a growing robustness and strength inside you. The relationship you have with the contents of your life verse is one of honor and obedience. A life lived with a life verse as its background bears continual evidence of God's presence, repeated confirmation of the power of God's Word at work.

Living under the influence of a life verse, we learn to think redemptively, live blamelessly, speak lovingly, worship cheerfully, pray genuinely, and serve faithfully. The steady application of God's verse for you turns you into a faithful follower. A life verse protects us from believing that life is up to us, reminding us we belong to a bigger story—a story we cannot abandon, because the moment we do, life becomes small, limited to only what we can see, understand, and reason.

Your life verse reshapes meaning, brings healing, and changes your outlook. Your life verse calls you to make new decisions about your point of view.

Produces Content

> He brought us out from there in order to bring us
> in, to give us the land which He had sworn to our
> fathers. (Deuteronomy 6:23)

The emphasis within this verse is God and His work. From the time of the Exodus, God became the content of Israel's faith.

Immediately after crossing the Red Sea, Moses offered up a song of worship celebrating the work of God's faithfulness. Before there existed any theological understanding or exegesis of God's great names, before Israel's and our traditions were formed, there was a confession born in the heart. Moses and Israel intuitively knew God's faithfulness, that He was a God who kept His promises and they were God's people. The Exodus story was the source of their creed. The emphasis of a life verse is always on who God is and what He has done.

Your life verse operates as a living word. It makes sense of your past, telling you who you really are and how you are to experience the present. Day by day, as Israel lived with and retold their life verse, their faith was informed and reinforced by God's character.

Your life verse will reveal three things about the character of God:

God Is a Liberator

Israel had begun as slaves in the hot brickyards of Egypt, where no future seemed possible. Since slavery was always about the task of the moment, they had no history or future, and the ways they were treated smashed any seeds of hope for another life.

For the Israelites, building Egypt by the sweat of the brow seemed the least likely place for a positive future to begin. There was no compassion in the brickyards. But the unexpected happened—God heard their cries and answered mightily. Time and again, God shows Himself to be a liberator, more than capable of freeing any captive.

> The LORD showed . . . signs and wonders before our eyes against Egypt, Pharaoh and all his household. (Deuteronomy 6:22)

This is where the plagues come in. The ten plagues were used to expose the empty lure of Egypt's idolatrous culture. God was not just focused on getting Israel out of Egypt but also getting the Egypt out of Israel. Four hundred years of being bullied by Egyptian power and greed had crushed the hope out of them and seduced them into believing the Egyptian way was the only way. God had to liberate their thinking so they would be free to follow in His ways.

God hears, He sees, He moves, He delivers, and He liberates from enslavement when freedom seems impossible. Today God liberates relationships and restores marriages. He sets students free from the opinions of others. He liberates the hurting from the trap of bitterness. He takes action to bring unexpected freedom in the midst of desperate, hopeless situations.

Powerful enough to overcome, compassionate enough to hear, and concerned enough to intervene—that is who God is.

There is a God who liberates.

God Is a Lover

God took action, not out of obligation, but out of love. The definition of God's mission to Israel was love. He was not willing to rest until Israel was back in His presence. He spoke to them in life verse when He said in Jeremiah 31:3, "I have loved you with an everlasting love." His character is the perfect blend of power and love; He is at the same time strong and tender. He is driven by His affection and will not quit until His people have reached their land of promise. God loves us, and all of His actions are performed out of love. God longs for His people to be restored.

We have confidence because we know He is faithfully, lovingly seeking us. He keeps at it even when we don't notice.

God is loving even if we are not.

The love of God becomes visible especially through the life of Jesus. Jesus delighted to show God as being full of love, sparing nothing for redemption. He came to the outcast, the rejected, the sick, the lame, the blind, and the demon-possessed, and He made them whole. He still intervenes to end estrangement and to draw the lost into a new spiritual family. God's love is not an ancient dream or a forgotten promise. It's a verb—a present, ongoing action.

God Is a Life-Bringer

God has the power to turn chaos into creation, to transform dark into light. His Word brings life to those who will listen and respond with trust. God is the one who can call into being the things that do not exist. And in Jesus, God acts as life-bringer for us, the walking dead. The Crucifixion was death's last effort to have its way, but the Resurrection opened up an exodus for us all.

When believed, a life verse has a way of freeing us from the old way of viewing life.

When you study your life verse—in light of its whole-Bible context—you'll discover that all these things are contained.

Protects from Compromise

Israel's history was one of broken promises and failure. When the people thought Moses had disappeared—he was actually in extended conference with God, getting a little document called the Ten Commandments—they placed themselves in jeopardy by departing from God and fabricating a golden calf to worship. They turned their affection and worship to an idol, which was a clear and blatant breach of faithfulness.

Every time the people of Israel turned their back on God, it was for one reason: They forgot their true story.

They let go of their life verse.

One of the benefits of your life verse is that it reminds you that your life is not your own; at the center of your story is God as your deliverer. When we forget our life verse, we will drift into compromise. Without a life verse we are in danger of derailing.

As a second benefit, a life verse protects us from small-mindedness, from reducing our journey to finding the next spiritual buzz or using God for personal entertainment.

And third, a life verse protects us from being self-dependent, taking over the work of the Spirit and using our own efforts to produce spiritual progress. The very presence of a life verse keeps us from making life about us and our effort. It keeps us from attempting to be know-it-alls and do-it-alls.

The good news is that it's never too late to recover your story and allow yourself to be reshaped. When we listen to our life verses and hear God's message of newness, God gives back our story, and as with Israel, we find our way back to Him.

Choosing God's story over our old story means that life can be reshaped and recast to a journey of hope. So, to make a long story short: His story is better than yours.

CHAPTER 7

The Birth of a Life Verse

NOT EVERYONE grew up going to church, but I did. Not everyone goes to a cool, hip, trendy church—I sure didn't. I was never a part of a life group, small group, cell group, or community group. There were no groups of any kind there. I was in Sunday school, but I didn't sign up or join—I was conscripted.

As I write this, I'm sitting in a hotel lobby because I can't remember what I did with my room key. But I remember every detail of Sunday school. Inside a neighborhood church on the second floor was a room where my class met. I held my mom's hand as we walked down that hallway and into the classroom. The air was filled with the smell of glazed doughnuts, the walls were painted the same shade of green used in psych wards. We kids sat in a circle of metal folding chairs around our teacher, who held a large black Bible open on her lap and who told us the stories of Moses, Joshua, and David and Goliath.

Every Sunday I listened to those stories, not realizing the learning process had begun. I had no idea how these narratives of faraway places would serve me later in life. Even though it was my young, short-attention-span heart that absorbed them, the lessons of those faithful men and women of Scripture would resurface in adulthood. To this day, I return to those stories again and again, and I've highlighted them in every one of my Bibles.

The words of Scripture have the power to mold you forever.

Maybe you didn't go to church or community group for whatever reason; your parents didn't take you, you got busy, you got offended, or you were wrecked by a crisis of doubt. As you read this chapter, allow yourself to begin the learning process now. And as you encounter one of those amazing Bible stories, consider that the answers for your personal world are found in another world—the world of Scripture. Where the impossible happens, where life is formed and reformed by its living words, where old lessons lead to new ways of seeing and being, where all that's needed is that you keep an open mind and heart. Not open to just anything, but open to God's amazing reality.

The Virtue of a Verse

It makes me think of one particular story in the Bible where a servant articulated the concept of a life verse so well: "May it be done to me according to your word." Such beautiful surrender to a disturbing announcement.

These are the words Mary spoke in Luke 1:38, when she'd just found out from an angel that she was going to give birth to the Savior of the world.

Mary's life would never be the same. Her plans for the life she had dreamed of were now completely undone, yet she met the words spoken by the angel with humility, confidence, and expectancy. The legendary response of this young woman was not born in the moment; it was not bland, pitiful piety or ritual religious action. Mary's response was not what one would expect from a teenage girl. It went counter to the beliefs of her culture. This was a time before a girl, unmarried and pregnant, would be given a prime-time reality show. Pregnant by an unknown father, she was in danger of being ostracized or even killed.

Her response wasn't passive or fatalistic. Instead, she welcomed the overshadowing work of the Spirit. Something else had already taken place in Mary, a prior birth. The birth of a life verse. We learn this about Mary by her response in song, which gives a structure for understanding the elements of the birthing of a life verse. Mary's prayer makes it clear that she already knew the Word of God, His ways, and how He speaks.

Where It All Began

The town where Mary lived had a strong synagogue ministry where the Jewish priests would gather to study the words of the Old Testament—the Jewish Bible. Studying God's Word was a regular part of life for Mary, whether because of tradition or devotion. Days, months, and years of listening to readings from the Bible accumulated in Mary's heart and mind, the words informing her and the other hearers with a deep sense of history—God's story. For Mary, the Scriptures were more than a gathering of facts from the past—Scripture was saturated with the way God always works, carrying out His promises, saving His people, demonstrating His loyalty. The sacred writings never tried to playact or pretend; they clearly and unapologetically stated the ways of God: how God dealt with His people, and how men and women responded to Him. God was living, forever and everywhere demonstrating His love and compassion by working His plan and calling His people to faith-fueled obedience.

For Mary, the Scriptures were not philosophy; rather, the ancient texts were filled with names and places inhabited by God, with real people in ordinary life, all of which revolved around God. Mary was filled with unshakable confidence in the continuity of God's plan, even to the present day, and she harbored no doubt that she was now privileged to participate in His work. This was her cue for her part in the play of the ages: enter Mary, stage left.

She was familiar with the history-infused lines of God's Word. She knew of the women of the Old Testament who had experienced miraculous births—women like Sarah, Manoah's wife, Ruth, and Hannah—all of whom had conceived and given birth in impossible circumstances. However, her birth announcement differed from the examples in Scripture; while the women of the Old Testament desired and longed for a child, Mary's was unexpected. What made it possible for Mary to surrender to this announcement?

Here are four components in the birthing of Mary's life verse.

Conceived in the Word of God

Mary didn't need anyone else to explain this situation to her. She was already so supernaturally aware that she herself interpreted the significance of the situation in words drawn from throughout the Old Testament, but applied in a fresh way. Mary's prayer, her hymn of praise, reveals her dependence on God's Word.

Mary's prayer wove together phrases and images found in the Old Testament. Mary treasured the Word of God and sang a song of collective biblical text. I encourage you to read her prayer in Luke 1:46-55, and check all the footnoted cross-references you'll find there to see how much Mary drew on her scriptural heritage.

Years of studying Scripture had trained Mary to see life with absolute honesty, but Luke is careful to point out Mary "treasured" the words and events, "pondering them in her heart" (Luke 2:19). *To ponder* implies a careful reading and a serious attitude, which enables an understanding of the Word that brings about obedience. Keeping the Scriptures before us acquaints us with the vocabulary of God. Filling our minds with God's Word heightens our sensitivity to truth. For Mary, the words she had read and treasured took on new insight when they came in contact with her circumstances. Her knowledge of the Scripture was put to work in the present, and a life verse was born: "May it be done to me according to your word."

Participation is required. When sitting before the Word, we are to read and receive. Then the Word conceives life in us and a life verse is birthed. His Word shapes our inner life; it's necessary to our formation. In reading God's Word, we become fertile ground for a life verse to sprout and grow within us.

Confirmed by the Wisdom of Others

There would be those who would gossip about Mary. She couldn't help hearing the talk in the town about her. She was not yet married, so surely there were suspicions of what might have happened, whether the baby was Joseph's or someone else's. Even so, Mary held fast to her life verse.

Fortunately, Mary was not alone. Her story was intertwined with another pregnancy, that of her older cousin, Elizabeth. Mary journeyed to Elizabeth's house for confirmation that what was happening to her was of God, and Elizabeth, by then six months into her own miraculous pregnancy, confirmed, "Blessed are you among women, and blessed is the fruit of your womb!" (Luke 1:42).

Once we have discovered our life verse, it's wise to seek confirmation. It's no accident that Elizabeth's husband, Zacharias, was a priest; these were godly people, so it was from this God-believing couple that Mary sought confirmation.

Too many times believers can take a verse out of context, twisting its meaning to meet their own needs, so it's vital that we look for confirmation of our life verse, not only from the context of the Bible, but from others. Many believers have misinterpreted a verse only to end up living in error, perhaps even bringing harm to others. We must be willing to defer to the input of godly men and women who can either confirm or correct our life verses.

If your life verse is God-spoken and God-initiated, the confirmation of others can keep you from thinking you are crazy or just hearing voices. God uses people to fulfill His life verse for you. Sometimes people will bless your life verse with words, and other times people will play a part in bringing the promise of your life verse to fruition.

A life verse will always bear the nature of Christ and will never violate the content and principles of Scripture. Your life verse should be confirmed by its consistency with the whole story of Scripture. Many times we can be too vulnerable to voices of the culture or to our own needs and selfish desires. We need not be too proud to seek the confirmation of others; there's wisdom in a multitude of (wise) counselors.

Created Mary's Life Foundation

Whatever had come Mary's way, her response would have been, "May it be done to me according to your word." There's a relationship between Mary's song and its scriptural predecessors, hymns of praise sung in response to God's intervention. These were the voices that informed Mary's life verse.

Moses, Miriam, Hannah, Deborah, Asaph, and of course, David—all are people who responded to God's call by singing praises.

In celebrating this moment, Mary drew from the memory

of God's activity in the Old Testament. She understood that her life was part of a continuous story. Through Mary's prayer, we enter a world of people who knew God as the foundation of their life, experiencing God fulfilling His word, making promises and keeping them.

For Mary the Scriptures were not merely an intellectual object to be analyzed and dissected—they were the foundation of her love, desire, and delight. The words she had heard were meant to be lived. Let me remind you that the being conceived inside Mary was Jesus, who from the beginning was and is the Word made flesh. This baby was the convergence of God's eternal plan, and Mary's response was the source of her willing obedience.

Your life verse is meant to be lived, just as Christ—the Word made flesh—can become flesh in us, the members of His body on earth. We make the Word flesh when we choose it as the foundation of our lives, lived practically. The Word becomes a light to our living.

As you read this chapter you might be in a workplace, a high-rise, a loft, a condo, a house, or a coffee shop. Look around and consider this: Every structure has an understructure—the building's lower, unseen part. The foundation. Most of the time, we are not aware of the foundation of a structure; people seldom ever look at a house and remark, "Hey, great foundation!" It's just there, supporting, upholding, providing continual support.

This is how a life verse functions—it supports your life. No matter the circumstance, situation, or problem you encounter in life, your life verse should surface in those moments. It's not something we self-consciously do; a life verse is a gift. We can receive it, respond to it, and practice it. And when storms hit, tearing at all the visible parts of a dwelling, you know what's left? The foundation. God's Word won't fail you.

We don't try to intentionally make the life verse fit into a life because so much of the work of a life verse is done below the surface, like a foundation of a building. We accept it, rest on it, submit to it.

Crafted Mary's Concept of God

God was never distant, never an impersonal authority. For Mary He was personal, not just giving out directives but showing her who He was. The most important aspect of discovering a life verse is that we are brought into contact with the One who gives it. Mary knew God to be a relational God; whatever words were spoken to her were personal to her.

Mary recognized God as the deliverer—*her* deliverer. He was *her* "Mighty One" who "has done great things" and who demonstrated His strength in *her* life. He was the God who went to battle for His—and *her*—people. He would prevail against His—and *her*—enemies.

Mary recognized the God of compassion. He looks with favor on His humble servants, lifts up the lowly, and extends mercy "toward those who fear Him." He acts "in remembrance of His mercy," always remembering His promises.

Mary's view of God was that He was a God of both combat and commitment.

Can you imagine what Mary sounded like as she prayed?

Imagine her telling God she loved Him, tears streaming down her face; the more she worshipped, the more the words of Scripture spilled from her heart and activated the glad surrender of her life. Imagine a time like this in your life. What words would spill from your heart? How many of them would be inspired by God's Word? How would your thoughts and prayers be influenced if you had already become convinced that your God is a conquering God? A God who is always present, who cares about you personally?

In that life-altering moment, would a life verse come to your mind? Might a life verse even be born in that moment, based on your familiarity with Scripture? The birthing of a life verse impacts our concept and relationship to God in three ways:

> *It fills our thoughts with the will of God.*
> *It expresses the emotion of God's heart.*
> *It cultivates relationship with God.*

Paul described just such a relationship with Christ—a relationship in which a life verse might be birthed—when he wrote, "I have been crucified with Christ; and it is no longer I who live, but Christ lives in me; and the life which I now live in the flesh I live by faith in the Son of God, who loved me and gave Himself up for me" (Galatians 2:20).

Are you regularly ingesting God's Word, gaining a familiarity with Him and His heart? Are you consistently entering with boldness into His presence? When you do, the soul breaks open and all God's words in your heart may flood onto your lips. Throughout her life, Mary had not only heard the Word—she had received it. It's imperative to become and remain open to whatever it asks of us. James warns us, "Prove yourselves doers of the word, and not merely hearers who delude themselves" (1:22). Nothing will take the life from your life verse quicker than not living in obedience to its words. May you be able to echo Mary and say, "May it be done to me according to your word."

CHAPTER 8

The Ultimate Life Verse

THERE WAS A FOCUS to Jesus' life—a reason for everything He did and said. While others around Him lived for themselves, His life was set on a higher plane. Jesus didn't drift through life or just let it take its course; He was a man on a mission. So how much did Jesus know from the start? Did He have a general idea about what He was to do and just make it up as He went along? This is the way many believers follow Jesus today—pick and choose, take what you like, and leave the rest. Was there more to Jesus' way than this?

Specifically, did Jesus have a life verse to guide Him? In order to answer this question, we have to know the role of Scripture in His life. He believed in the authority of His Bible, which during His time on earth was the Old Testament. He quoted it as the basis for marriage; He drew upon the story of Jonah to explain His resurrection; He used Scripture in times of temptation—when confronted by the Enemy, the Word was His arsenal. Jesus could have said anything, yet He chose to use the Scriptures. His life was saturated with the Word of God.

Jesus' disciples all believed the Hebrew Scriptures to be authored by God, setting forth His plan for the redemption of mankind. The authors of the New Testament believed reading the Old Testament was the same as hearing God speak. They held to the conviction that God's Word couldn't fail because God Himself couldn't fail, assured by the confidence that His Word will stand forever and will never return without accomplishing its task. The writers of the New Testament used the words of the Old Testament extensively and wrote under the infallible guidance of His Spirit, meticulously recording what God spoke for them to write.

The people of the New Testament church viewed the entire Old Testament as confirmation of Jesus Christ. Jesus fulfilled what the Old Testament predicted; His life and work were seen to be the work of God—the very representation of God in the flesh.

We've seen that Jesus believed in the Scriptures. He knew that the words defined what He came to do. But did He have a life verse? Since all of the Old Testament points to Him, could we say all of Scripture served as Jesus' life verse? Maybe. But was there a specific verse that shaped and summarized His whole life? Once again, to answer that question, we have to go to Jesus' life setting—one day in particular—and watch how He interacted with God's Word.

Take the Passage Personally

The synagogue that day was crowded; people had come from nearby towns to see the local man—a former carpenter whose newfound fame as a rabbi had spread throughout Israel. The growing crowd was waiting with eager anticipation to hear what He would read and how He would apply it afterward. The roomful of locals was ready to listen. Jesus stepped up. The crowd grew quiet. Every eye was fixed on Jesus. The attendant handed Him the scroll. Jesus unrolled it, opened His mouth, and spoke the lines He had selected:

> The Spirit of the Lord is upon Me, because He anointed Me to preach the gospel to the poor. He has sent Me to proclaim release to the captives, and recovery of sight to the blind, to set free those who are oppressed, to proclaim the favorable year of the LORD. (Luke 4:18-19)

He gazed intently at His listeners, then gave the scroll back to the attendant and sat down.

Jesus had just read His life verse aloud.

These words, from Isaiah 61:1-2, would determine and define Jesus' ministry. What made them so subversive was not the words themselves, but that He was so brash as to take personal ownership of them.

The Side Effects of a Life Verse

> All the people in the synagogue were filled with rage. (Luke 4:28)

Sitting down to teach was customary in that culture; it meant Jesus was about to address the crowd. I have to say that as a speaker myself, having stood in front of many crowds, my instincts for addressing an audience might have been to open with a clever story or an encouraging remark, but Jesus did not do that here. His listeners might have expected Him to remind them of their great Exodus story, but Jesus didn't do that either. Instead He bluntly, straightforwardly brought the Word into the here and now. In no uncertain terms, He assured this synagogue full of people—with whom He had grown up—that the kingdom had arrived:

> Today this Scripture has been fulfilled in your hearing. (Luke 4:21)

The blind were gaining sight, cripples were walking, lepers were being cleansed, the deaf were restored to hearing, and the dead were being raised back to life. The implication was clear: Jesus—their little Yeshua—was Messiah.

The audience was amazed at His words. He spoke with inner conviction, freshness, authority, and the listeners were impressed. But quickly their amazement turned to rejection. Jesus' audience pushed back at the words He had spoken. "Is this not Joseph's son?" they said. Basically, *Who does He think He is anyway?*

When Jesus quoted Isaiah's prophecy and then claimed to be its fulfillment, He linked Himself to the actual bringing of salvation. The implication was crystal clear —a new era in history was dawning. He was setting the old way aside; now the door of salvation would be open to all comers.

But there are side effects to living by a life verse. Not everyone is going to appreciate it, and there will be push-back. This is one of the unavoidable truths we draw from this text.

The words of your life verse will create disruption—not just with others, but in you, too. The verses that Jesus read would push Him into conflict with friends, battles with evil, and ultimately His final suffering on the cross. Without this verse, Jesus could have stayed quietly in town and continued to teach. But to be sure, this was *not* Joseph's son. In following His life verse, Jesus chose a destiny that would lead Him through hardship on the way to glory.

At first our experience of discovering our life verse is filled with wonderment and an atmosphere of adventure as we explore God's Word. We fall in love with its words of blessing and the promise of its full dimensions. We delight in its wisdom, and even commit some of the words to memory to give us comfort through the rough patches.

But sooner or later we all find that our life verse will make us uncomfortable. Discovering one's verse is affirming and appealing—and then comes the discovery that the verse and the book from which it comes were not meant for our entertainment.

Like Jesus' life verse, our life verses make demands of us. Within our life verses are hard things, costly choices of obedience to be made. Looking at life through your life verse, things appear strange; they may even seem impossible to conceive as being real. At first we want a life verse for comfort; when it ceases to feel comfortable, we are tempted to adjust it or to abandon it and go find one that is. But all life verses are linked to a bigger story; we quickly reach a point where we realize that we can't tell our life verses what to do for us. To do so would be like cutting flowers off at the stem, leaving them without a source of nourishment. Imagine lifting a verse from the page, cutting it off from its source, and wearing it like a corsage; it's pretty, but disconnected from the life-giving flow, it dies.

Your life verse comes with the whole Bible as its context. And all that that implies.

Jesus' life verse thrust Him into a story of action, and it does the same for us, too. We don't get to decide the outcome or the part we play in the story. We are not given the luxury of making it up as we go along. Instead we let the text speak to us and about us, telling us what to do. The ultimate side effect is that we are never again the same.

Full Scope of a Life Verse

The Spirit of the LORD is upon Me. (Luke 4:18)

Jesus summarized every aspect of His message and ministry when He read this passage. This verse immediately recognized that Jesus' life would never be fulfilled apart from the supernatural will of God. More than philosophy, these words from Isaiah formed the bond between Jesus' words and actions. We see teachings of the kingdom interspersed with demonstrations of healing, recovery, and freedom for captives.

Jesus' life verse produced an intense focus, and as a result, Jesus never wondered what to do with His time. The Spirit of the Lord was on Him. Through the work of the Spirit, He was given supernatural capacity to bring justice and righteousness to the world. The Spirit defined His ministry; His words brought about spiritual and physical changes, His touch resulted in freedom and released His work. He was establishing the kingdom, all while making the presence of God obvious on the earth.

Yes, Jesus had a life verse! It defined His whole life. Through His ministry, Jesus would communicate His life verse in different ways: "The Son of Man has come to seek and save that which was lost" (Luke 19:10), or "I came that they may have life, and have it abundantly" (John 10:10). All His work flowed from His life verse—healing the sick, raising the dead, teaching on a hillside, hanging out with sinners, confronting religious leaders . . . Every action of Jesus was tied to His life verse.

A life verse gives a fresh vision for the future and sets the tone of one's life. The compelling nature of a life verse helps us navigate some of the most difficult and challenging circumstances of life. While we cannot control the choices of others, a life verse can help in the way we respond to others. The life verse also becomes a guide by which we filter situations and set boundaries with others.

Your life verse will both inform and inspire you to follow in the way of Jesus. Apart from the Word, we tend to live by emotion, the whim of the moment, or others' opinions and ideas. Basing your life guidelines on Scripture rests your life's task in God's heart. His Word is eternal and never returns without accomplishing its intended purpose. It's received in the present as if it has already been accomplished.

We must not think of our life verses as something that may or may not happen. When the author of Hebrews says the Word is living and active, he means in the present; it requires that we respond to what's being said, never postponing it or putting it off to a later time.

Your life verse addresses *all* the responsibilities of life in *every* season of life. Nothing is out of the reach of your life verse, including your job, hobbies, interests, relationships, diet, debt, or community involvement. A life verse doesn't compartmentalize life.

A life verse is also linked to the past while looking to the future, giving you a grasp of reality. It's easy to assume that a life verse is magic, that it will make everything better all at once. Indeed, all of God's Word is supernatural, but it works through your commitment and obedience. We have to live in active response to God's Word; through your life verse, God is entrusting you with your part of the work to be done and the choices to be made.

A life verse involves the senses. The mind translates thought into images, like when one's memory recalls events from years ago in living color and with great detail. Let yourself experience your life verse using all of your senses. What does your life verse look like in the physical setting of your life? How does it feel to live the truth of your life verse? What do your words sound like as you give voice to your life verse?

Does it change your conversation or the way you speak to others who have hurt you?

Living a life verse involves everything unique about us: our history, our relationships, our failures, our secrets, our faithfulness. A life verse doesn't tell us to run from our life or present us with a command to try harder. Instead it sends us into life saying, "Live into this."

God's Help with Your Life Verse
Because He anointed Me . . . (Luke 4:18)

Jesus began His ministry after being anointed by the Spirit; the Spirit is the "because" of Jesus' work. Note that there are no records in the Gospels of Jesus preaching and teaching until after the Spirit had descended on Him (Luke 3:21-22). Then Jesus was led by the Spirit into the wilderness (4:1-13), and it was after returning in the power of the Spirit to Galilee that He began His ministry with this proclamation of His life verse (4:14-15). The capacity given to Him by the Spirit wasn't for personal amusement or enjoyment—the Spirit was on Him because He had an assignment.

Simply put, all Jesus did was powered by the help of the Spirit. Jesus drew attention to the fact that He would not do anything without the presence of the Spirit. For Jesus, this had always been the case; indeed His whole life had been accompanied by the Spirit. All accounts make it clear that the Spirit's work was essential to His birth, His identity, His warfare against the Enemy, and His ministry. Jesus experienced the power of the Spirit, making evident that His life verse was at work. Jesus thought of His life in terms of the Spirit. His awareness of the Spirit and being used by the Spirit were the keys to His effectiveness.

Similarly, we are not left alone in this world with a handful of words and sentences—a life verse with no spiritual backup. A life verse cannot be experienced without the help of the Spirit. A life verse has its own gravitational pull, drawing the help and the resources of God to fulfill it.

The test of how you're handling your life verse is whether you have a greater dependence on Jesus—that's the hallmark of the Spirit. Whenever our conduct branches off from the work of the Spirit, we end up living in delusion. A life verse faces reality, lives in the present, and always points us to Jesus.

Your life verse is not a Roman candle, lighting up the sky one minute and gone the next. It is there to shine on your way day after day. God provides His Word as an eternally burning light for our feet and a lamp for our path (see Psalm 119:105).

Often when a person goes adrift, tossed around by impulses and the culture, God can seem vague and distant. Life can feel like marching in place. Discovering your life verse brings a compelling vision for life and connects you to the help of God. Your verse contains a target, an assignment. God plans to put you to work, so there is direction to your verse. And for your life verse to be effective, it must have the help of the Spirit. Your life verse is more than a trinket; it's God's Word made real through the help of God.

Just as it took the involvement of God's Spirit in creation, moving over the face of the waters to form the earth, your life verse cannot be lived apart from God's Spirit. Jesus offered people a compelling vision of what life would look like with the help of the Spirit when He said, "With God all things are possible" (Matthew 19:26).

> *Describe what your life could look like if you believed the Spirit was presently at work in you.*

> *What do you desire more of in your relationships? In your work?*

God's Grace in Your Life Verse

. . . to proclaim the favorable year of the LORD. (Luke 4:19)

Jesus' life verse concludes with the phrase "the favorable year of the LORD." This is a reference to the Year of Jubilee, which every fiftieth year was to be a year of release, in which debts were canceled, slaves were freed, and people who had sold their property because of poverty received it back. The Year of Jubilee began with the sound of a ram's horn blasting through the air to announce the good news.

The word *proclaim* carries the same connotation. No longer would the sound resonate from a ram's horn—rather now it was the words of the Anointed One, blasting into this captive world, that would announce the arrival of grace and a time of release. They would signal freedom from condemnation through the work of the Messiah. The year of God's favor is still in force today and will continue until His coming.

Though Jesus quoted His life verse from Isaiah 61, He left off part of it. (He can do that; He's the Author.) This was not from carelessness nor because He ran out of time. It was intentional. He closed His life verse with "the favorable year of the LORD" but omitted "the day of vengeance of our God." Jesus' listeners would've assumed the favorable year of the Lord meant the cancellation of debt—followed by God judging their enemies. But judgment was not yet present! Witness the wonderful wildness of God's mercy upon all outsiders, outcasts, enemies, and renegades, giving them every chance to receive the redeeming work of God.

Jesus had come to deliver people from judgment and every kind of opposition. Jesus lived with an expectation that people would be saved and set free to experience the power and liberty of the kingdom, and most of all, to know the love of the Father.

Your life verse is never a word of judgment or wrath; Jesus took those on Himself at the Cross.

Your life verse sees something good about you that maybe you have not seen. Inside every life verse is an expectation of good, of success. Your life verse is always tied to the character of God. As we make our way through life, we encounter sticking points—times when we get stopped. We have to go back to the One who spoke the Word of the life verse. Those words aren't just nouns, verbs, and adjectives—they communicate heart, meaning, energy, and truth.

Go back and listen to the heart of the One who spoke those words.

> *Have you been listening to a voice of condemnation that has been holding you back?*

> *What has that voice been telling you to do or not to do?*

> *What obstacle do you need to overcome in order to believe God's Word?*

> *Is some circumstance or individual trying to get you to deny God's Word?*

PART III

CHAPTER AND VERSE: READING FOR YOUR LIFE VERSE

MY LIFE VERSE has taken a lot of beating. Over time its value to me has increased. The events that led to my discovery of my life verse began in my family. I was the only child of my mom and dad. Both my parents were hard workers—my dad a plant manager and my mom a teacher. My dad worked the late shift, then stayed out late and came home even later. His night friends, along with many self-destructive hobbies, began to pull at the seams of the marriage, and soon the union was ripped apart.

My dad moved out and moved on. As the years passed, school got tougher for me and my grades showed it. My confidence took a blow. If I was called on to read aloud, I felt so much anxiety that I broke into a cold sweat. Tests were a struggle; the questions caused my mind to go blank. None of my teachers knew what the problem was. Nor did they have time to figure it out.

So I was labeled a slow learner—one who had no hope of an educational career. I was isolated from the student body. My days were filled with specialized classes, tutoring clinics, counseling, and therapy. All the experts reinforced the labels. And labels have a way of sticking and shaping stories.

One of my mom's coworkers noticed what the others had missed. When I wrote, I printed letters backwards. She recognized I had dyslexia. This was an obstacle, not a death sentence. I discovered that I learned differently from other people. But I *could learn*. It was a slow and steady process, but I pushed on.

It was during this season that I experienced the unflinching faithfulness of God. I also discovered something else— my life verse.

During my season of discovery I began reading the Bible. Because of my fear of reading, in the past I had stayed away from the Bible—as I had from most books—but I remembered that Deuteronomy was a book about the faithfulness of God and Moses' final words to a new Israel, so I thought I'd check it out.

I was a slow reader, but as my eyes took in the words, the words became sentences and the sentences formed into thoughts. I would read some, then stop, then come back and read some more. I read Deuteronomy for months. Many times, upon returning to the book, I would have to remind myself where I had left off and what had just happened. But my reading pace didn't matter. I simply read and listened.

I read and reread these words, all the while whispering

this prayer: *Lord, let Your Word come alive to me.* Every time I opened the Scriptures, I imagined I was stepping through a door and into a world with an atmosphere of authentic emotion, thoughts, and events. I became a participant, a genuine seeker and learner. The more I "walked around" in this world, the more I discovered. I was surrounded by the verbal reality of the deep loyalty of God.

Then it happened.

Something reached out from those pages and grabbed hold of me. I was aware there was a sudden shift in my reading, and the words that had pulled me into the past world in Deuteronomy were now alive in the present. I was face-to-face with a verse whose context I knew from the long weeks of reading. But now these specific words suddenly sounded personal. It was as though they were speaking right to me. There they were on the page, except now they also broke over me like a wave.

I was looking at my life verse.

> Nevertheless, the LORD your God was not willing to listen to Balaam, but the LORD your God turned the curse into a blessing for you because the LORD your God loves you. (Deuteronomy 23:5)

This verse fit all the standards of a life verse. It summarized my life. It gave the past, present, and future events of my life a redemptive focus. It proclaimed the gospel and connected me to the faithfulness of Jesus. These words were alive and active in my present tense.

It was a while before I would read the remaining eleven chapters of Deuteronomy. I spent more than just a few days in that verse; I spent *months* reading and rereading those words, listening and letting the verse soak into my life. A slow intertwining of text and life took place.

While thinking of my life, I would look at each part of the verse, and amazing insight came to me.

. . . not willing to listen to Balaam . . .

Here's a little backstory: Balaam was a soothsayer hired by Balak to speak curses against Israel in an attempt to derail their future as God's people. In three attempts, Balaam was mysteriously stopped every time. His words had no effect. In fact, try as he might, all Balaam could do was proclaim blessing on Israel.

When I think of all the destructive and misleading labels that had been slapped on me by others, I'm surprised that their malicious power could not deter God's plan for my life. He surrounded me with spiritual Teflon.

. . . turned the curse into a blessing . . .

No evil words spoken by others can corrupt the heart of God. What incredible assurance! I'm not surprised this is my life verse, because it's perfect for a dyslexic. Usually life looks like it works against us, but when God reverses curses, they are turned into an advantage. In my struggle with reading, I tapped into creativity I didn't know was there.

Besides my fears of reading aloud and writing, I was also terrified of public speaking. But if you have read my bio on the back of this book, you know I've spent the last twenty years doing the three things I thought I could never do! I've been operating in what I believed to be my three greatest weaknesses.

My life verse taught me that my limitations can never limit God. My life verse has shaped my message into one of hope and change, which God has used to challenge and inspire thousands of students and adults.

. . . because the LORD your God loves you.

God's love is one of commitment, along with fierce loyalty to act. His love is not just one of desire, but of action. In this verse notice that "love" is a verb. God does something about our condition, our restrictions, our curses. We are in a relationship with God, who is caring toward us and who actively intervenes on our behalf. So when I look at life through my life verse, I'm constantly reassured that God's curse-changing power was not exercised solely in the past but is still at work in the present. And this helps me walk into an uncertain future with confidence.

My life verse has gotten better with time. I'm thankful for everything God has done—for each turnaround, for each insight, for the steady doses of hope. I will not get mired down in the memories of the past, but will continue to listen to and live out my life verse.

✦   ✦   ✦

If my story has encouraged you, just think how your story might encourage others. Please visit YourLifeVerse.org and tell us your life verse story.

CHAPTER 9

How Do You Read?

How DO YOU get to May Avenue? Believe it or not, there is more than one way to answer this question.

Directions according to my GPS:
Merge onto I-77.
Go 2 miles north, exit right to 122nd.
Turn left on to 122nd.
Go 2 miles east, turn left on Hefner Road.
Turn right on to May Ave.

Directions from a senior adult: Well, let's see, you get on the turnpike . . . now that didn't used to be there. [Scratches head. Thinks.] It was originally a two-lane and nothing but farmland on either side. At the time, the city hadn't come this far out. Years ago I guess they put a highway right there.

Anyway, you get on there. As you drive you'll see
a lake. On your right there's a park there . . . and
jogging trails. [Looks off into the distance.] There
didn't use to be. Originally it was just a lake, but they
really have developed it now. Well, you exit at 122nd
and turn left and then . . .

Where did you want to get to?

Directions from a woman: Head toward the mall.
As you drive you'll see the cutest row of shops on
your left. Keep going. On your right there are some
discount clothing stores, a fun little house with
yellow trim, a shoe store, a beauty supply store, and a
nail place. Turn right there. You'll pass a party shop,
a stationary shop, and a beauty salon. [Spots a mirror,
touches up lipstick.] Oh, and of course when you see
the dress store, you've gone too far. Turn around and
head back a block to the cupcake shop.

Directions from a teenager: Uh, it's somewhere over
there. Head that way. You'll probably see it.

We have a natural tendency to give directions through personal filters based on personal passions, age, and stage in life.
The same is true when reading Scripture. Personal preferences, perceptions, and practices form our interpretation of
the text. To be sure, reading starts before the book's cover
is opened.

There's more to reading the Bible than just opening a

book, more than looking at letters on a page and knowing the difference between verbs and nouns. I've often heard sermons calling the congregation to read, just read. True enough, that's a good place to begin. But still there's more to consider. Placing a Bible in the hands of a reader and saying "Hey, good luck with that" is like giving a gun to a child. A great deal of wreckage has been created by faulty Bible reading. However, there must be a way to help readers get their bearings with the text.

I've attended many Bible study groups where the majority of the time is spent talking about each person's idea of what they think a passage means to them. Where every comment begins with the phrase, "Well, what I think the verse is saying is . . ." These circles of uninformed believers place Scriptures at the mercy of personal preferences, opinions, bias, holy guesses, and assumptions. We'd best not forget that the Word of God is living and active. The Bible connects us to the reality of a living God, His love, His salvation made visible through His Son Jesus. If we forget the aliveness of Scripture—worse yet, if we substitute our own insights, if we quit listening to the living words of Jesus, if we become unwilling to submit, unmoved by His love—an arrogant spirit is born in us. We try to master Scripture instead of letting the God of Scripture master us.

Reading Options

Scripture is written in a variety of genres—history, prophecy, poetry, narrative, parables, letters, and apocalyptic literature. Each has its own context and guidelines for interpretation, which help in our understanding of Scripture's original intent. There are many books available that explain each of these approaches and provide us with proper information regarding the author, time, place, and purpose of the books of the Bible.

Still, the ways we read are determined by more than a set of interpretive guidelines, study methods, or questions of authority. To address the question *How do we read?* involves examining the attitude with which we come to the book.

Back to the Book

In Luke 10:25-37, Jesus was confronted by a Bible scholar whose job was to read, interpret, and defend the law of God. He was serious about his work. He was knowledgeable, discerning, and defensive. He asked, "Teacher, what shall I do to inherit eternal life?"

This was not an innocent question. This scholar was out to trick Jesus and was going to use Scripture to do it. But Jesus would not be drawn into the scholar's game of gotcha. Instead He asks the scholar a question: "How do you read? Tell Me what the Law says."

The scholar answered accurately. There was nothing wrong with his knowledge of Scripture. Jesus acknowledged that he'd given the right answer, but there was something wrong with the *how* of his reading. The scholar read the text as a faithful Jew, a philosopher, and a lawyer. As one in control of the text. But something was missing.

His answer had included, "Love . . . your neighbor as yourself." And the man knew that he fell short of some interpretations of this command. So, in an attempt to justify himself, he added a follow-up question: "Who is my neighbor?" He was attempting to turn the truths of Scripture into objects to be debated, dissected, analyzed, and discussed. But Jesus' words pushed the scholar away from controlling the text for his own outcome. Jesus told the story of the Good Samaritan—a very practical, living application of Scripture. He was saying by this that God's words were not just material to be used to win debates; rather, to read Scripture properly is to *live* it. Jesus concluded His encounter with the scholar by giving him a command to *participate* with the words he had gained expertise over. Jesus told the scholar to go and *do*. To live out the text.

The same applies to us today; we read the Word to live. So now with every flip of the page we hear Jesus' question, "How do you read?"

Reading Like Jesus

Jesus' question evokes the question, *How did He read the text?* Certainly He was an expert in understanding, a spiritual genius. After all, He *is* the Word. During His earthly ministry, Jesus quoted from Scripture, He spoke it, read it, heard it, tasted it, and lived off of it. He called others who had lost their way to hear the heart of the Father in His Word.

How did Jesus read? He read Scripture as Jewish liturgy; He was handed the scroll and read in the synagogue in Nazareth. He read historically; He quoted from Moses, the Psalms, and the Prophets. He read theologically; on at least two occasions He called religious leaders to right understanding and observance of Old Testament teaching. He read prophetically; He taught His disciples the big picture of the Old

Testament as a framework for grasping His life and death. He read as a teacher; the Scriptures played a vital role in His formation and teaching. The value and depth Jesus found in Scriptures reverberates in the writing of the New Testament and the priority the early church gave to all of Scripture.

Jesus' reading was shaped by His experience of God. A few times in Scripture we are permitted to listen in on the private prayers of Jesus, particularly in His aloneness in Gethsemane. As we listen to Jesus pray, we hear Him use the word *Abba*. It's like *Papa* or *Daddy*. It is the spirit of the Son who cries *Abba*.

The Jewish culture of Jesus' day regarded God as "Father"; for most this was an intellectual concept, a formal address. But by calling God *Abba*, Jesus revolutionized our understanding of God. *Abba* was more than a manner of addressing God; it was expression of His own experience with God. With fatherly care, *Abba* cared for Jesus as an individual. Jesus' experience of God was not common in His day. The Presence that Moses could not look upon, the God who dwells in clouds and unapproachable glory, was addressed tenderly, intimately as by a child sitting on his daddy's lap. Jesus' experience of God was so full, so creative that it found voice in the word *Abba*. Jesus had an unusual, unprecedented intimacy with God. To Jesus, God was so real, so loving, so compelling that in His prayer His cry of *Abba* filled His speech.

In light of this experience of God, Jesus' reading of the Scriptures involved two components: relationship and response.

Reading in Relationship

Jesus was aware of His sonship with God. It held particular importance in His life. He often spoke of Himself as the Son of God. We are given insight into His relationship with God as Jesus explained it to His disciples.

All things have been handed over to Me by My
Father; and no one knows the Son except the Father;
nor does anyone know the Father except the Son.
(Matthew 11:27)

Jesus claimed to have divine knowledge of God that only a son could have of a father. His understanding of God flowed out of His personal intimacy with Father God. He knew God in a way no man ever had. This was not an intellectual or philosophical idea, but His experience of God's approval toward Him. Throughout His ministry, Jesus emphasized His son-to-father relationship with God. He testified, "The Son can do nothing of Himself, unless it is something He sees the Father doing; for whatever the Father does, these things the Son also does in like manner. For the Father loves the Son, and shows Him all things that He Himself is doing" (John 5:19-20).

It was Jesus' understanding of God as Father and of Himself as Son that influenced how He read Scripture. His sense of sonship enabled Him to read and apply passages from the Old Testament that gave Him inspiration and ideas that shaped His mission and ministry.

Upon Jesus' baptism, God spoke, declaring, "This is My beloved Son, in whom I am well-pleased" (Matthew 3:17).

Then in His temptation in the wilderness, the Devil twice challenged His sonship: "If You are the Son of God . . ." (4:3,6). And Jesus replied to the Enemy by quoting Scripture as God's Son. Throughout His ministry He would often say, "You've heard it said . . . but I say to you . . ." Then He would make fresh applications of the Scripture, all driven by His sonship. Jesus had an original mind and a new spirit unheard of in His day. As a son He took old common ways of thinking and recast them afresh, using Scripture in new, revolutionary ways. All in light of His sonship, His connection with God in the closest relationship of love and obedience.

Reading the Bible is like reading a letter or a card personally addressed to us. A mom who knew she would not live to see her daughter become a teenager wrote a letter:

You are the greatest thing that's ever happened to me.
Your life has given me something I will never lose.
You've brought love into my life, a love that will
never fade. I admire your courage. There's never been
anything you couldn't conquer. As I've watched you
grow, you've inspired me. Your energy to learn, read,
and write, to share deep thoughts. Your passion takes on
new things—to sing and dance and act. I'm surprised
daily with all the beautiful things that are in you. You
are a few months away from being a teenager. I want
you to know how proud I am of the girl you are and the
woman you will become. Keep your courage up. Live
life to the fullest.

Love, your mom forever

This letter reveals a relationship—one formed and bonded in love. What is amplified in the words of the mother is her heart, her care, her strong belief in her daughter's destiny. The intimate, life-changing power of this letter, throughout the seasons of the daughter's life, will never disappear. This is precisely the kind of relationship we have with the text of Scripture. We, like Jesus, read God's Word as family members.

The relationship Jesus had with the Father, He encouraged His disciples to seek and cultivate as well. To those who have decided to follow Jesus, He says there is a deeper experience—one that goes beyond following God at a distance: to know God as *Abba*. Jesus cast a new vision for God's relationship with us. This relationship begins with our repentance and the commitment that brings forth the fruit of repentance. Then, by willingly following Him in action as well as in word, we can experience the fatherhood of God. The Spirit who cries *Abba* makes the believer a son and a fellow heir (see Galatians 4:6-7).

To reveal the heart of the Father, Jesus told the story of the prodigal, who after a season of riotous living came to his senses and returned to a father who was looking for him, had prepared a place for him, and ran to meet him with open arms. This is the *Abba* Father whom Jesus knew and encouraged His listeners to know.

Reading in Response

Jesus' *Abba* relationship with God was not a fantasy or a means of escape from reality. For Jesus, *Abba* implied a deep surrender and a willingness to fulfill the demand of the Cross. The Father made known the mission to the Son, and the Son accepted. It's fascinating to realize that Jesus didn't start His ministry with a job description or a list of titles He wanted to be known by. Rather, Jesus started with His sonship, which in turn brought direction to His mission. He did nothing on his own—only what *Abba* told Him, whether it was eating, preaching, teaching, or healing.

Why does sonship matter in your discovery of your life verse? Because without an understanding of our sonship (or *childship*, if you prefer the gender-neutral term), the reading of the text can be cold and detached from reality. Discovering your life verse doesn't begin by having perfect theology or a complete understanding of Bible history. It begins when we read Scripture as a letter written to us by a family member who loves us deeply, sacrificially. Reach out. Pick up a Bible. And open it as you would a personal letter or card from a dear loved one. Reach for the Scriptures with the same intensity and focus with which you check a text on your phone. Open the Book with same anticipation as you open an e-mail from a close friend or loved one.

As far as God is concerned, if you're in Christ, you're a family member, you've been fully forgiven, you are completely loved, and the lines of communication are clear between you and Him. God has more to say to you about your relationship with Him. He's written you some letters and sent you some texts to more fully express His heart to you. Do you have to understand everything about a letter written to you if you know the heart of the one who's writing? Does it matter if the word structure does not always make total sense? If someone were to write you a love e-mail in broken English, would that lessen its intensity and meaning for you?

How do you read? Most of us don't read as theologians, historians, or philosophers. Those are highly specialized categories that require formal training. Most of us begin reading from a different place. The same place where Jesus prayed, lived, read, taught, and ministered: as a son. That's how we read.

CHAPTER 10

The Way
of the Ear

RECENTLY, through a series of events, it was pointed out to me that people are bad listeners. I know this is not a particularly profound discovery. Be it at church or social events, we don't listen. We don't ask questions about the other person's topic, we don't nod with attentiveness when he or she speaks—we just wait our turn.

It's not pleasant to be alone on the sending side of a one-way "conversation." At one time or another we've all experienced the frustration of trying to communicate something of importance, only to feel as though our words were disappearing into thin air and, based on our listener's response (or lack of it), realizing our message wasn't heard. Sure, the words bounced off the other person's eardrums, but he or she wasn't really paying attention to our meaning and so interpreted what we were trying to say through his or her own perspective.

A while back I was interviewing a pastor about speaking and writing discipleship material. We both took seats in his office, he behind his desk and me in a subordinate position across from him.

I greeted him. "Hi, I'm Dave."

He replied, "Oh, nice to meet you, Dan," then embarked on a fifteen-minute gloat-fest, telling me how great he was. And then he paused before saying, "Well, enough about me. What would you like to know about me?"

I wish I were making this up.

We love to hear ourselves talk. For most of us, listening is just various forms of controlling our inattention until we can get the subject back to us. We have several strategies for doing this—several forms of fake listening. Let's take a look at them.

First, there's *clickening*, which is the art of enduring long phone calls about people and places you care nothing about while trying to conceal the sound of your mouse clicking on different websites or the intense game of solitaire you're playing.

Rant listening—a common skill developed among couples—is letting the other person rant about some insignificant incident so this ridiculous story doesn't make it out into the public.

Another common form of fake listening among friends is the *trade-off listening*—in other words, "you listen to my hour-long diatribe about an uninteresting part of my life and I'll listen to yours," though sometimes the party who goes first skips out on his end of the agreement. He talks, then walks.

Still another form of nonlistening is called *pseudo-interest*—that is, nodding and maintaining eye contact with the speaker while at the same time making a mental list of tasks to do after he's finished.

This failure to listen is one of the basic causes of relationship problems. If it hurts our natural relationships, then it will certainly harm our spiritual connection to God.

Heeding Means Hearing

So, what's this got to do with finding a life verse? Reading the Bible is about listening. Sounds simple. It's not, mainly because we're not used to listening when we read God's Word. The difficulty is that we often read for information, not for application to our lives. Experiencing Scripture was never meant to be segregated from the rest of life; rather, the life in the pages of the Scripture is to intertwine with our own lives and have a say in our conduct.

The answer to our struggle with Scripture is not just learning more information but listening.

And we are not good listeners. The challenge lies especially in listening to Scripture on its own terms, the way God originally intended. When those words were first spoken and written down, they were life-generating, forming and shaping the people who listened. So why shouldn't they have the same effect on us? Indeed they should and can. This "new" way of reading actually takes us back to the way that most people throughout history have typically received God's Word. Listening to Scripture is compatible with the way it was written, especially because most people *didn't read*

Scripture back then. They couldn't. Paper was expensive and literacy was rare. The people who heard Scripture *literally heard it*. Read aloud.

In order to get it in them, they had to *listen*. And they couldn't listen selectively. They couldn't skip ahead when they got bored. The listener wasn't in charge of the process; the voice of Scripture was. And so God's Word struck the listener with an authority that we often don't heed or respect.

Reading as an act of listening centers on life change rather than amassing information, and finding your life verse means reading to live. This is a different way of approaching the Bible, allowing the text to come alive, truly absorbing the words and appreciating the weight they carry.

You might not be aware of this, but you already possess this skill.

Think of a time you and a friend were talking. Perhaps he or she said something that resonated with you, and in response you said, "I hear you." This implies you heard something that wasn't literally spoken; you perceived the person's full intended meaning; you knew that what the person meant was more than the sum of the words.

A person reading with a real openness to life change enters into an experience of "redeemed hearing" that perceives the meaning beyond the words. This person, with the help of the Spirit, picks up on the holy intent of what the text is saying. This kind of listening is what the writers of the Scripture were concerned with: being in a receptive state, listening to be changed by the text.

One of the tangible ways we experience this is in the

process of discovering one's life verse. Listening to the text, we are moved out of our ordinary way of living and become engaged with God, who is, after all, the Author of each believer's life verse.

The writers of Scripture constantly challenged their readers to listen:

Incline your ear and hear the words of the wise. (Proverbs 22:17)

Give ear and hear my voice, listen and hear my words. (Isaiah 28:23)

Your ears will hear a word . . ."This is the way, walk in it." (Isaiah 30:21)

He who has ears to hear, let him hear. (Matthew 11:15; see also 13:9,43; Mark 4:9,23; 7:16; Luke 8:8; 14:35; and more)

Clearly, the writers weren't speaking only of physical ears. Physical ears alone don't hear the living voice in the words on the page. We are to listen with ears of our hearts, to let the living words of the living God form and change our lives. Then we no longer read just to get an idea or to feel an emotional buzz; instead the Word permeates our lives and brings insight. A light comes on, a sudden flash, followed by knowing. An "aha moment" or whatever you want to call it.

We get the inside scoop on what God is doing, not

through the eye, but with a hearing ear. All our reading is ineffective without listening to the words spoken by a personal God, words taken personally by us.

Hindrances to Hearing

Speaking of communication, I face a challenge in my own life. My phone service carrier offers little-to-no coverage. Getting a signal on my phone is determined by several factors, like not putting my hand over the antenna, holding my head at the proper angle, and standing on one leg.

Just as there's an art to sending and receiving calls on my phone, there's an art to hearing the Scriptures, and there are factors that can interfere with the signal strength between our "ears" and God's Word. God's Holy Spirit plays an important role in this process. Here's how Jesus put it:

> When He, the Spirit of truth, comes, He will guide you into all the truth; for He will not speak on His own initiative, but whatever He hears, He will speak; and He will disclose to you what is to come. He will glorify Me, for He will take of Mine and will disclose it to you. (John 16:13-14)

We must be aware of five hindrances that can get in the way as the Spirit helps us hear God's Word:

Noise

Music, news, podcasts . . . There's so much noise in our lives that it's hard to hear what's important. And the noise isn't all external. We also experience constant interference from frantic, anxiety-driven thoughts, static due to selfish desires and motivations. God is like the rest of us—He doesn't enjoy being interrupted, especially when He's sharing something personal. Letting the noise interfere with our connection to God is, in effect, like cutting Him off midsentence. However, in cultivating calmness and quiet, we find hearing God is much easier.

Secondhand Theology

More often than not our so-called "knowledge" of Scripture is based on what we've heard or overheard in a particular religious environment, spoken by people who have promoted a set of ideologies rooted more in tradition and history than in the Bible. The life-giving truth of the Scriptures can be obscured by our presuppositions. We need to come willing to challenge our assumptions.

Inherited Ideas

All of us come into our lives with patterns of thought, behavior, information, and beliefs that have been handed down. These ideas develop into safe, predictable comfort zones. Often this makes reading the Scriptures difficult; we read through the lenses of other peoples' ideas, distorting the heart of God's Word.

Prejudging

This means unreasonable bias or opinions contrary to the facts. Really, *prejudging* is just another word for prejudice.

Our prejudice breeds suspicion, intolerance, and hatred, be it against race, gender, class, or status. This can be a blockade to hearing and receiving the words of Scripture. We aren't intended to read Scripture to shore up our inclinations— rather we read as sons and daughters of God to understand our Father's heart.

Things I Like

The things we like in life aren't necessarily bad. But often these good things—pastimes, habits, skills, lifestyle, aesthetics, entertainment—become blind spots, keeping us from welcoming the unfiltered truth of God's Word. The God of Scripture doesn't submit to personal preferences or entitlements. We don't read to get our ways approved by God, but to be captivated by His gospel.

The good news is that overcoming these hindrances doesn't have to be a lifetime struggle. They can be disarmed, for starters, by setting the Scripture in front of you and simply asking God, "Lord, help me to hear."

How to Hear

So how do we go about listening to the text? Let's examine four elements. These are not necessarily steps or a formula— instead, listening to Scripture involves the integrated motion of all four working together; like a hair braid, each element overlaps and intertwines with the others. The strands are repeated in sequence until finally the finished product forms something of beauty. Moving through these elements enough times forms a way of living, producing a rich inner life of insight, and among other things, leading you into hearing and living your life verse.

These four strands are designed to awaken our ears to the point where we are moved by what we hear, where our reading of the sacred text draws the response, "Ah, I hear You." What follows are instructions in the way of the ear, based in part on the commonsense wisdom of Proverbs 2:1-5:

> My son, if you will receive my words and treasure
> my commandments within you, make your
> ear attentive to wisdom, incline your heart to
> understanding; for if you cry for discernment, lift
> your voice for understanding; if you seek her as
> silver and search for her as for hidden treasures; then
> you will discern the fear of the LORD and discover
> the knowledge of God.

Examining the lines in this proverb brings insight and instruction about training our ears to listen.

Let Go—"Make Your Ear Attentive" (Proverbs 2:2)

Opening the Bible begins with opening our spiritual ears. Following a formula is not required; rather, it's about tuning in with an attitude of anticipation. God is waiting to meet you! Our attentiveness is sharpened by knowing God's Spirit is going to speak to our spirit. The Bible is not the end, it's the beginning that serves as a launching pad into the presence of God.

It's important to remember we are not meeting with words on a page—we are encountering the living Word: Jesus. We are not seeking an encounter with a book. It was not a book who lived, died, and rose again; it was not a book through which all things were created—it's Jesus, who is the living Word. The written Word of God always leads us to the living Word of God. His presence is what we are becoming attentive to.

Achieving a listening state means reading what is written the way it's written on the page. Reading the Bible on its own terms means letting go of reading our favorite passage or jumping to conclusions about a specific interpretation of a verse. We must first let go of our personal preferences.

I once spoke at a conference in New Mexico that featured a different speaker each night. My spot fell midweek. I spent some time that day with the program staff, catching up on the speakers who had gone before me. I asked what topics they had covered, and one person said, "Oh, the parables. We've heard that stuff before."

Assuming the point of a text is already known to us because we are familiar with it—that's a sure sign we are not in a listening state. We are so skilled at having all the right answers, so polished at predicting the outcome of a passage of Scripture, mistakenly believing we know what to do with it. Premature certainty can clutter a person's ears with the sound of his or her own voice.

We have to let go of our "expertise," telling ourselves we know all we need to know. Using our knowledge of the text to confirm what we already know by bringing our preconceived ideas and predictable answers makes reading Scripture boring. It's time to stop reading to be correct and start reading to be changed.

It's in our own best interest to listen to Scripture with a sense of wonder, which can be lost when we use the Bible as a simple answer book, a security blanket, a good-luck charm, a magic eight ball, an object upon which to swear in court, a moral referee, a set of proof-texted absolutes, a collection of doctrinal statements, or evidence to win arguments. Approaching Scripture with a predetermined set of expectations flattens its depth, making us tone-deaf to what really is being said, bypassing an encounter with a living God.

Letting go means ridding ourselves of the burden of trying to control words, trying to strong-arm a meaning out of a text, forcing it to meet our standards. Instead, each of us must begin by becoming available as a partner in a conversation. Making the ear attentive begins by realizing God longs to be present to us.

We pay attention when someone we value is saying something important. We face Scripture openly with clear ears. Begin by getting back to its original intent: What was the Spirit saying when these words were first spoken or written? Then the text surprises, energizes, and enlivens. Letting the Scriptures speak from their context frees them to become a source of faith, a launching pad to encountering the Word.

A life verse is born as a result of sitting before the Word with attentive ears tuned into the text. It's not done by tearing a verse away from its context and using it any way we please; nor by telling the text what to say or pressing it into our assumptions. Rather we listen and let the Word speak.

EXERCISE

Letting go of your assumptions about the text, read the verse below slowly, letting your eyes rest on each word. Now listen, allowing yourself to be drawn into the verse.

> *Above all else, guard your heart,*
> *for everything you do flows from it.*
> (Proverbs 4:23, NIV)

As you read, did a word or a phrase grab you? Do you sense any new insights being formed apart from the old way you might have perceived this verse? Simply bring yourself before God in silent consideration.

Consider the word "guard." We are to put ourselves in a place of watching, to be aware, on guard. By watchfully guarding you are able to keep your words, thoughts, and desires in check.

What comes to mind when you read the word "heart"? How is it to be valued? What does that imply?

Lean In—"Incline Your Heart to Understanding" (Proverbs 2:2)

In the above-quoted instruction from Proverbs, the teacher challenged the student to put to use his full capability; the ear is to be used to hear the Word afresh, the heart is to *apply* what is heard. We're moving from looking at words of the text to entering the world of the text. The world of God is more vast than our minds can comprehend; the words of God are meant to draw us into greater insight into God Himself.

The Bible is made up of stories of people strong and weak, fearful and courageous. Some lived in places surrounded by beauty while other locations were desolate, and they faced events both tragic and victorious. They experienced suffering, rejection, loss of life, loss of hope. There is a connection between all the stories in the Old Testament and the New—all encountered a saving, blessing, working, moving, life-giving God.

All these stories share a context—namely, God at work in His world.

Engaging the Scriptures, we discover a personal, relational God entering into the lives of real men and women. Leaning in or inclining the heart means entering the world of God. Leaning in means giving the text attention, rehearsing, dwelling diligently, considering, noticing how the verses you are reading are connected to the rest of Scripture. Leaning in helps us to see the truths in the text that were not visible on a casual reading. Leaning in opens up the wide world of God's Word to show us how all the stories connect.

Leaning in guards against us taking verses out of context,

proof-texting, and isolating verses by twisting their real, intended meaning. Leaning in places us in the world of God's self-disclosure. Not an indulgence in escapist fantasy, leaning in makes full use of our imagination by allowing the places, the people, the words they spoke, and the God they encountered to come alive to us. We stand next to Moses as he listens to the voice in the burning bush; we take the long journey up Mount Moriah with Abraham and Isaac; we run to the tomb with the disciples and discover with them that He is risen.

Leaning in is participating.

Leaning is an act of friendship. When a good friend begins to share something private, disclosing life, becoming vulnerable to you, your natural reaction is to pull yourself to the edge of your seat, focus all of your attention, and soak in every word spoken and every emotion shared. You're totally engaged with the person being revealed, seeking complete understanding by entering into his or her world.

Though all the stories of Scripture take place over a span of thousands of years, the unifying component is Jesus. He is the context for every text. From Abraham to the apostles, all saw Jesus in the words of Scripture. Every page of Scripture reveals the Savior, and leaning in makes us aware of the connections.

By leaning into the text, we meet Jesus there.

Your life verse is from another world, the world of God's Word, where all the stories emerge from one coherent story. Your life verse takes on a whole new meaning when you lean into the story it is a part of. Your life verse is grounded in a historical faith; it cannot be understood apart from the entirety of Scripture. Careful study of Scripture is essential; it serves in grasping the big story. Entering the world of God's Word requires reading a book in one setting to gain a sense of the sweep of the story.

Leaning into the world of your life verse brings about spiritual formation. The goal of reading the Bible is not to finish a book but to meet with God. Reading for depth means remaining open to whatever God has to say.

EXERCISE

To help develop the skill of leaning in, take this verse through the key elements of leaning in. I'm providing you with a different Bible version of the verse in each of these exercises, in order to give you varied and fresh perspectives on it.

> *Watch over your heart with all diligence,*
> *for from it flow the springs of life.*
> (Proverbs 4:23)

First, let go of whatever you already think this verse means. Read it slowly several times. Consider the content.

Now tune your heart to Jesus' presence by leaning in to listen. Read again. Now pause and wait patiently. Remember, you're not here just to learn facts, but to lean into His presence. Think of Jesus walking you through this text. Don't allow your thoughts to wander. Your attention is no longer on things around you. Now your mind and heart become occupied with the text you're reading and with the One who spoke it.

Consider the context: What are the cultural background facts of this passage? What was the teacher intending to communicate? Knowing this will help you more accurately perceive the world of the verse.

Now ask yourself, If I received these words in writing, personally addressed to me, what would they mean?

Now use your imagination. What do you see, hear, feel, taste, and smell when you read "flow the springs?" Of what does the flow consist? What might it be carrying? From where does it come? To where does it flow?

Add your own expression. How would you rewrite this verse to clarify and expand upon the writer's intended meaning? What imagery would you use?

Lift Up—*"Lift Your Voice for Understanding"* **(Proverbs 2:3)**

The word "lifting" in this line of Proverbs means "to give." After leaning in and working our way into the world of the text, embedding it in our hearts, we are to lift it up in prayer.

Prayer is a conversation, not a monologue, and when you're lifting up, the topic of conversation is God's Word. We take the message we receive as a result of our reading, and we give it back to God in prayer.

Prayer is made up of words, and here the words we pray are based on Scripture. We not only hear and understand God, we speak to Him, we ask, we argue, and we question. Yes, we argue and question, because it helps us achieve deeper understanding and personal application. And besides, He can take it. Reading the Scriptures followed by praying the Scriptures—these are essential to discovering our life verses.

When detached from Scripture, prayer becomes a short-circuited conversation. God is revealed in the Scriptures that we read and meditate on, giving both form and content to our prayers. We pray the Word, because prayer gives us entrance into intimacy with the heart of God, which is represented in the words we read.

God doesn't reveal His Word merely so that we can grasp it intellectually and move on—our insight increases as we pray and participate. Praying Scripture—especially your life verse—keeps you responsive to the Spirit. Reading alone leaves us with heads full of knowledge and empty hearts.

We pray what we read, working our lives into active participation with what God reveals. God's Word is not meant to be inactive but to be lived in real time, to be taken personally.

Are you listening? Can you hear the Word inviting, commanding, challenging, calling, directing? Praying the Word is your answer.

EXERCISE

Read this proverb again, and as you read, take it in carefully, taste it, digest it. We tend to read Scripture quickly, going from one verse to another with the goal of finishing a chapter. To pray Scripture, we must read it slowly. Stay focused on this verse until you sense the heart of what you are reading.

Keep vigilant watch over your heart; that's where life starts. (Proverbs 4:23, MSG)

Let Scripture lead in your prayer. Craft the words and meaning of this proverb into an offering to God. Read it slowly in His presence. If new insight comes as you read and pray, or you become especially aware of the presence of Jesus, stop reading and remain still. Let God do in you what He will.

Prayer is the outpouring of the heart. Using this Scripture, write a personal prayer. Let it be heartfelt and God-inspired. The goal of this exercise is not to make a list of needs, but to

pray this Scripture with the help of the Spirit.
Give up your own desires and requests. Let
everything around you dissolve, and let the
Word lift up your heart.

Live Out—"Then You Will Discern" (Proverbs 2:5)
Now that you've thought on and prayed through the Scripture,
the final element in the process is living the truth in real life.

The way the Christian life is often presented today, it
seems to be tailored only for certain personality types, like
those prone to solitude. The new spiritual hero is a kind of
urban monk, who, with the exception of his designer coffee, leather-bound journals, and cutting-edge technology,
delights in being secluded from the world and its amenities.
He is an introspective in pursuit of going deeper.

Then there's the type A Christian, who loves to take tests
on everything from spiritual gifts to personal strengths. She
loves to set goals for her spiritual life and measure her progress.

I'm not criticizing either of these ways of living, but there
exists another category, called "the rest of us." Those of us
who live lives filled with noise, who deal with the demands
and expectations of others, who handle the daily grind of
everyday life, always juggling relentless duties, family, and
jobs. It's the everyday Christian who struggles with weakness,
who loses his temper, shoots her mouths off, feels regret, gets
confused, fails diets, breaks promises, becomes distracted,
and sometimes feels just plain clueless.

That's me, anyway.

No matter which category you identify with, the goal is

the same: We all assume the task of living out what we read. We all seek a life formed by God's Word—listened to, prayed through, and lived out. This is not a life only for introspectives or type A's—it's for anyone who wants to follow in the way of the ear. For those who want to live what they've listened to. Living out means allowing the truth we've read and heard to run its course. And we live without fanfare or being preoccupied with "looking Christian."

Scripture—and particularly your life verse—can only be lived in love. It's not something we do out of our human ability. We can read, pray, and think, but it's only by love that real living—living God's way—takes place. Living it out happens when reading, listening, and praying converge into being aware of the life we are living. The first three alone are not enough—we are called to live the text in Jesus' name.

EXERCISE

Read the proverb again, slowly, a few times.

> *Guard your heart above all else, for*
> *it determines the course of your life.*
> (Proverbs 4:23, NLT)

What's your immediate re-*action* to this verse? (How does it prompt you to act?) Is it a command or an optional choice? Is there a duration of time we are to watch over our hearts? What motivation does the verse give for obedient action?

Try to imagine yourself without faults or
failures; it's the redeemed version of you.
This version of you lives out the heart
meaning of Proverbs 4:23 in every situation,
perfectly.

Think backward: Place that version of you in
a situation you lived yesterday—a situation
you wish you had handled better. How does
that version of you respond? What kind of
choices do you make? How do you speak? As
you play this mental movie, you are creating
a redeemed picture of your day done a little
better. It's a kind of rehearsal that can become
reality next time you encounter a similar
situation.

Now think forward: Picture yourself continuing
through the next twenty-four hours with Jesus
present beside and inside you. He's working
with you in each moment to guard your heart—
watching over your words, resisting outbreaks
of pride, dissolving moments of hate and
selfishness, holding you back from careless
decisions. When you mess up, you will admit
it, you will ask and receive forgiveness,
and you will keep living the next moment in
dependence on God's Spirit.

When you see these envisioned changes in
your life, you'll know you're following the way
of the ear. You're listening to God's Word.

Hearing as Habit

This way of living must be cultivated into a habit. Practicing
these four strands and letting them shape the way we read,
listen to, and pray through Scripture will form the image of
Christ in us and craft within us a fresh, clear way of hearing
God through the text.

> *Let go*
> *Lean in*
> *Lift up*
> *Live out*

As you develop these skills, you'll find that you don't always
have to lock yourself away and wait to hear God. You don't
always have to set up the perfect quiet time. You'll develop
these skills so they become instinctual every time you open
God's Word. Every time you open the Scriptures, lean toward
Him with a heart of trust and love, and these things will
come with greater and greater ease.

The primary way to discovering your life verse is hearing
with your heart. This means that all of your reading is done
with a spiritually receptive heart. As you set yourself atten-
tively and patiently before the open Scriptures, what will
follow is what I call the pop of the page.

CHAPTER 11

The Pop of the Page

ONE NIGHT I was attending a dinner with some friends. The crowd was about forty people, and I didn't know everyone, so I milled around with my friends, occasionally meeting and greeting the people I didn't know. I was introduced to a doctor and his wife, and we exchanged hellos. Intending to make small talk, I asked the doctor how his day was. "Did you see a lot of patients?" I asked.

He warmly replied, "Yes, as a matter of fact, I did. I treated a case of moderate to profound rhinorrhea paroxysm diaphragmatic irritation-impeded conjunction." I had no clue what he'd just said. His medical-speak made total sense to him but none to me.

I didn't know what else to do, so I looked to his wife for an interpretation. She said, "That's a runny nose and blood-shot eyes with cough."

"Ah, yes," I nodded knowingly.

He continued, "I also treated a case of maxillary and ethmoid fullness with swollen erythematous boggy turbinates."

Again I looked to his wife. She kindly said, "Earache."

The doctor, unfazed by my inability to follow, continued. "And I had a few cases of pyrexia anterior and posterior cervical lymphadenopathy, which was probably due to a subtype of coxsackiervirus."

By now we had a rhythm—I heard his words but needed help on the interpretation. His wife once again made it plain. "That's a common cold."

I shouldn't have asked, but the question leapt from my mouth before I could help myself: "What do you prescribe for those sicknesses?"

"Diphenhydramine, phenylephrine, dextromethorphan, acetaminophen."

Before he was finished, his wife said, "Nyquil."

From time to time, we all need help figuring things out or getting a clearer meaning on a project or assignment. Anyone who has ever tried to assemble furniture, bikes, or toys knows the feeling of confusion when trying to make sense out of the instructions. It's even more disturbing when there are pieces left over after assembly.

Reading the Bible is like my encounter with the doctor. I knew that I didn't understand the words he was using, but thankfully I had someone there who would interpret his technical jargon so that I could still engage in the conversation. When reading Scripture, we are looking at words spoken and written in a different language at a specific time to a certain culture, and often the meanings of the words don't translate easily into our language and our modern world. So we stare at pages of unfamiliar words, phrases, and references knowing those words are important but not getting their full impact.

You are not the only one to struggle with reading Scripture. Acts 8:26-40 chronicles one episode in the spread of the gospel to those who had never heard it before. Philip had received a divine command to travel south to Gaza, which led him to the Ethiopian eunuch, a Gentile. This Ethiopian man was seated in his chariot—which likely looked like a covered wagon—with a scroll of Isaiah spread out in his lap, reading its words aloud.

The Spirit instructed Philip to approach the Ethiopian's chariot, and as he got closer he could hear the man reading the words of the scroll. Philip shouted out a question: "Do you understand what you are reading?"

It's Okay to Ask for Help

The Ethiopian man asked Philip to join him in his chariot. This man was open and honest about his lack of understanding. It's better to be humble about your lack of understanding and know-how than falsely overconfident.

So few are willing to ask for help, nor are they willing to open up and listen. This is why, for many, reading Scripture is lifeless and boring. Understanding the Scriptures is not like working a sudoku puzzle, where by logic and effort we just get the numbers in the right place. The fact is, God has given us His Scripture along with the help to understand. God sent Philip to the Ethiopian man to help explain and apply the words he was reading; how wonderful that he didn't wave Philip on with a "Hey, I got this" nod, but instead was humble enough to ask for help.

The passage the Ethiopian was reading was Isaiah 53:7-8, the prophecy of the suffering servant, which had been fulfilled in Jesus. Now there's no evidence that anyone in first-century Judaism had been expecting a suffering servant, but rather a triumphant Messiah. It was Jesus who applied this passage to Himself when He referred to these words in Mark 9:12.

The passage in Isaiah doesn't contain a lot of detail about the person who would fulfill this prophecy, which makes help from an outside source all that much more necessary. So the Ethiopian sought help by asking, "Please tell me, of whom does the prophet say this?" (Acts 8:34).

Philip knew, so "beginning from this Scripture he preached Jesus to him" (verse 35). It's important to remember that not one line of the New Testament had been written yet. Philip used Isaiah to reveal the story of Jesus to one who did not know Him.

Then There Was a Pop

And suddenly there He was! Jesus in the Scriptures had come alive and found a place in the Ethiopian's heart. The change in his life did not result from a vision or an epiphany—it happened as a result of reading and understanding Scripture. The truth had popped off the page and taken effect in this man's life; the Spirit of God had given this man joy, courage, power, and a new message to live. There was more in those words than just history—there was the living Word, Jesus.

The pop of the page can happen only with some outside help. Philip's story is careful to specify that Philip's role was directed by the Spirit of God, who used him as an unusual messenger to make the unseen known. Philip shows us that the pop happens as a result of the Spirit of God giving insight into what we are reading.

You may discover your life verse when you see a particular Scripture pop off the page; the words on the page jump out from their original context and become a living voice. There is far more involved in listening to a living voice than reading a written word; the passage becomes personal. With some help, the verse for your life pops off the page and something registers with you through the words of that verse. A part of Scripture spoken and written long ago during a specific time in history to an audience of foreign listeners now applies to you.

That's how you know it's your verse.

Your verse puts life in perspective.

Scripture doesn't pop off the page by accident. A few basic attitudes have to be set in place first. Those attitudes shape the way we read and help us know what we are looking for. They heighten our sensitivity to the text. To experience the pop, we have to sharpen our perception of the Word and become open to the Word being formed within us.

Let's explore the basics that enable the pop of the page.

Don't Forget What You Are Reading

When you look at a text on your phone, are you reading and studying the phone itself, or are you reading words that express thoughts from a person? Hearing that buzz or ding—does it remind you to learn more about how the phone works, or do you instantly know you have a personal message from a living, breathing individual? The same is true with our Bible reading—we aren't trying to get to know a book, we're seeking to connect with the God of the book. This perspective matters because it impacts our view of the Bible and the Bible's ability to work in us.

Discovering your life verse doesn't happen apart from a right view of the Word of God. If we treat it as an encyclopedia of facts and figures, its meaning is lost on us. If used as a recipe book for "right living," the personal connection is all but nonexistent. If handled as a textbook, where its words are depersonalized, dissected, analyzed, and clinically debated, we become onlookers instead of participants.

The character of the one speaking matters, influencing the way we hear and interpret the words. We cannot expect to experience the pop of the page without accepting the Scriptures as the source of absolute truth, just as their Author is absolutely true. We must believe that the Bible has absolute authority in matters of faith and life, based on the Author's absolute authority. The Bible is more than a work of man—it's the inspired Word of God. God picked the writers, making sure they accurately conveyed the thoughts that He desired.

However our experience doesn't find its goal with believing in authority and inspiration. If our sole interaction is with the strength of the text, it places the Scripture in a position of being a bully, pushing us around because it can. We then perceive a kind of a dictatorial "do this because I said so" interaction with the text. Inerrancy, infallibility, and authority are not the be-all and end-all of our connection with Scripture. These three indispensible elements set us up for something greater.

Reading as an Act of Love

The Bible is given so we can know and love God. We need a high view of Scripture, but we also need to know the God of the Bible. There's the Bible and there is God. Understanding the difference helps us; as we read God's words in the Bible, we discover there is a relationship with God to be had. For this purpose, it might be helpful to think of the word *POP* as an acronym for the "Person Of the Page," the living God to be known, loved, experienced.

Our connection to the Bible is the God whom we encounter within it.

When we have a conversation, we don't say we had an inerrant or authoritative talk. No, we say we had a heart-to-heart, or we hung out, or we connected. We don't say, "I really got into those words"; we say, "I felt loved or heard or challenged." One heart meets another.

In conversation we encounter the soul of a person. Getting to the pop in Bible reading involves God telling us His story so we may "get into" His ways of thinking, feeling, and acting.

It's this attitude we assume when reading to discover our life verses. We read to connect, to communicate. And if we don't, we miss out on the pop.

Our reading must go beyond a mechanical approach, to

reading as an act of love. Such reading loves the One who speaks, it loves hearing and getting the words right, it loves enough to carefully listen, not just to scan the text to get the gist of it and move on.

Can I Get a Little Help Here?

Back to the story from Acts 8. The Spirit first directed Philip to travel in the direction that took him to the Ethiopian man and then again prompted Philip to stop and speak, opening a conversation that brought about the pop for the Ethiopian. The pop of the page is the work of the Spirit when, jolted by the text like a thunderclap, we see something we've never seen before and gain a new insight. What was once mysterious and unknowable suddenly becomes understandable and personal. The role of the Spirit in reading is not limited to discovering your life verse but is essential to your continual reading of the Bible. The Spirit helps us actively listen.

Bringing the Spirit into our interaction with Scripture radically alters how we experience the Word we are reading. When the Word and the Spirit are linked, our understanding is deepened and faith is stirred. Because of the work of the Spirit, the words that were revealed to writers long ago are again brought to life within the reader.

As we read, the Spirit takes the historical text and connects His Word directly to our present life. When the ancient text of God collides with our present, you experience a flash of clarity. You see the big picture and abruptly absorb instinctively, in a personal and visceral way, what's being said.

The pop of the page.

The Word and the work of the Spirit are intertwined. We must have an understanding of both.

The Bible functions in two primary ways: first as a historical text filled with people, places, and events; secondly, as an instrument of transformation. In the first way, we read the Bible, and in the other way, the Bible reads us. As we look at God's Word, His Word looks back at us and asks questions about choices, beliefs, and destiny. The Bible becomes the ground from which the Spirit speaks, making Scripture new and fresh, both inspiring and stretching us, igniting new possibilities for life.

As you hold the Bible, think of this: God has spoken. We are given the foundation of Scripture. The text is settled and we believe it to be the Word of God. However, the Spirit is fully engaged and still communicating, both bringing understanding of the text and changing the mind and heart of the believer. How do the Spirit and Word work together? Let's look at three ways.

The Spirit Helps Us Recognize the Word

No one knew more about the Spirit than Jesus. As we've seen, in His parting words to the disciples, He spoke of the work of the Spirit and the Word:

> When He, the Spirit of truth, comes, He will guide you into all the truth. (John 16:13)

One activity of the Spirit is to personalize what we read. Some truth is inward and spiritual, not understood by the world. This function of the Spirit is critical to the success of Christians. By the Spirit, first-century believers gained special insight concerning the words and works of Jesus. The Spirit still guides today, continually filling out the teaching and ministry of Jesus.

The Spirit Helps Us Interpret the Word

The Spirit is crucial to interpreting the Bible. Reading the Bible can seem dry, dull, and pointless. It's long, it's not arranged chronologically, and it uses a variety of literary forms that change from book to book—even chapter to chapter. All these things can be confusing, so let me simplify them: The Bible is about God. From creation all the way through, God reveals Himself to men and women like us, created to have a relationship with Him. Though the ability to know Him was corrupted by our failure, God has made a way, through Jesus, for us to enter the story and participate in the life of God both here and eternally.

With the help of the Spirit, the Bible makes sense. The Spirit awakens our imagination, and what once were old, far-away places and events in Scripture come alive with meaning.

The Spirit Helps Us Apply the Word

The pop of the page doesn't stop with insight. The Spirit takes the words on the page and turns them into the living presence of God speaking. God's story flows out of our lives through *application*. Sometimes applying Scripture can be difficult because, without the help of the Spirit, we only see in Scripture what we want to see. We read "Love one another," but it's the job of the Spirit to fine-tune these words by enabling us to love the unlovable. We read "Worship God," but it's the Spirit who helps us see driving peacefully through traffic as an act of worship. The outcome of reading is that our minds, wills, and actions are transformed. Good reading leads to application. If it does not, it misses the point of God speaking and preserving the Word. If the result of your reading the Bible is a changed life, then you are reading correctly.

The Path of the Pop

There is no set recipe for the pop of the page, but it always involves the help of the Spirit. Experiencing the pop is more of an art than science, and like artistic skill, it can be developed through practice and attention. You quietly set yourself before Scripture, always remembering it is the Word of God. Ask for the help of the Spirit.

Clear out a block of time and find a quiet place. The pop is more likely to happen with an uncluttered, unpressured mind and peaceful spirit. The more often you can be at peace while reading, the greater the potential for the pop of the page.

It's best to start reading Scripture at the beginning of a book. Don't be concerned with remembering all the facts, or gaining a perfect grasp of the material with your intellect.

Given this attitude of relaxation and reliance on the Spirit, you'll be reading along through Scripture and along will come a flash of awareness, a new understanding. You'll find yourself thinking, *Oh, wow! This has to do with me.*

That's the pop!

The page has become personal, God's presence has become real, and the Word will speak to *you*. Words you've read or heard preached many times before now become intensely and intimately *yours*.

Here are four pointers that can help you achieve the mental and emotional state I've been describing:

Stroll, Don't Stomp

If you have ever led a small group or a Bible study, you're familiar with the Saturday-night cram session to teach your lesson on Sunday morning. For me, it starts about nine p.m. I locate the curriculum, read over the material, then look up a few verses and hope for the best.

Cramming only retains information in short-term memory, and little change ever comes from it. Speeding through the Bible is like coming in the house with snow on your boots and stomping off the excess—assuredly not an effective way to recognize your life verse.

Discovering your life verse requires slowing down, taking time to absorb every word, to notice each meaning. We seek a rhythm of reading in pace with the moving of the Spirit. Keeping in steady time, we relax, read, and wait, then again relax, read, and wait. The goal is not to cover large amounts of text at once—you're not in a contest. Try strolling through Scripture, like strolling through a neighborhood or a store, letting the landscape of the text fill your vision.

Slowing down helps us submit to the text. Slowing down guards us from becoming cocky about what we've learned;

humbly waiting on God's Spirit helps keep our knowledge from puffing us up. Slowing down sifts out distractions.

There's so much to know from Scriptures; if we are moving quickly over it, we miss all the beauty. As you stroll you are giving a chance for the words to pop off the page.

Graze, Don't Gorge

I've never traveled anywhere in the Western world where people aren't busy. Most live their lives on the go, always moving from one meeting to the next, one errand after another. Meals are missed or replaced with snack food so that, feeling famished, we finally ingest one big meal, cramming food in at a rate that would make a pig say, "Whoa! Take it easy!"

Life habits shape our Bible reading. We might go for days without any Word, then read, go to class, and listen to a sermon all at once. Eating too much can make one bloated, and so can long periods of Wordless living followed by overstuffing on the Bible. A body gets fat because it can't metabolize all the food, so it shuts down, stores the calories, and breaks the scales. Live this way long enough and the heart suffers.

Jesus chastised the Pharisees for this very thing: "You search the Scriptures . . . and you are unwilling to come to Me so that you may have life" (John 5:39-40). They had overstuffed heads and undernourished hearts. The Pharisees spent hours every day reading, studying, teaching, and talking about Torah. Their way of life was taken up with the Word, but all the wisdom and knowledge stuffed into their heads bred only arrogance and pride. They worshipped their reading more than the God they were reading *about*.

They had failed to graze on the Word with the help of the Spirit, and so they ultimately missed Jesus. When these men had encounters with Jesus, they wanted to debate points of the law, personal heritage, and social justice. But they missed Messiah because the words they had long studied never connected with their hearts. He was standing right in front of them and they accused Him of being a demoniac and a false teacher.

Grazing gets us into a place of receptiveness. I can't say I've made a habit of watching cows, but I do know there's not a lot of movement to their eating. Herds tend to graze in specific areas, slowly chomping away. Reading Scripture has a similar feel. As you begin to read five to ten chapters a day, slowly move through them, waiting for something to pop off the page. When it does, stop there. Don't worry about finishing the day's assigned chapters; rather, carefully follow the steps covered in "The Way of the Ear" (chapter 10). If you feel there's more there to be discovered, then stay there longer. Be prepared to read an entire book in one sitting or to stay in one chapter or verse for long periods of time. Both long and short readings are necessary—the goal is to graze and slowly let the Word be absorbed into your heart.

Rest, Don't Run

We love tasks—so much so that the ability to multitask is seen as a virtue. I know several people who can simultaneously put on makeup, talk on the phone, send e-mails, and study for a presentation—all while driving.

Unfortunately, this mentality can find its way into our reading of Scripture. Spread out on a table before us are different translations of Scripture, commentaries, and four different Bible resources open on the laptop. Our eyes dart from the screen to the page, clicking frantically from one resource to another looking for a deeper truth. One of the most freeing things I've learned in regard to studying is that there comes a point when you have to close the websites and reference books and rest. You must simply sit, allowing a particular passage—perhaps your life verse—to soak into your mind and heart, letting it brew within you.

Too often it's our familiarity with the Scripture that hinders greater discovery of the contents of a verse, especially when we feel we already know what a particular verse or passage means. This is a clear indication we need to spend more time with the text. It may take a few days or weeks of patiently reading and rereading the verse, but resting makes it possible to know your verse at a more intimate level.

The manner of resting is up to you. Some sit on the floor while others may choose to sit in a comfortable chair. Some use music, because music can help open the imagination. Begin your resting time with prayer, asking God to take what you already know intellectually and help it become real to you. The goal of resting is, with the help of the Spirit, to help us experience Jesus as vividly as possible.

It's only as we cease from striving and rest in the unconditional love of Christ that our soul is nurtured by the truth within a passage. As we rest in total honesty, we give the Word a chance to work its way through the struggle points of life and connect us with the love of God, ultimately becoming a new motivation for living.

Just let Christ be Christ in you. Just rest in the truth.

It's in resting that we experience the healing and transformation of the inner life.

Stop and Stare

Committing your verse to memory is important, but it's just as important to get it into your imagination. Turn your verse into pictures. Imagine for a moment or two what your life will look like if you fully believed that verse. Dream.

The more you do with a particular verse—the more you think about it, pray it, talk it over, apply it—the more you'll remember the words. Focus on meaning first, and memorization will happen automatically.

The Proof Is in the Pop

This way of reading leads to the discovery of your life verse. As a result of knowing your life verse you'll be able to make better decisions, have more confidence in uncertain times, see new solutions to old problems, and enjoy a greater sense of engaging God. The path of the pop is simple, but it takes a bit of effort to get to the place where the way of the ear becomes natural. If you'll connect with Scripture with a clear mind and a calm heart, remaining receptive to the help of the Spirit, you will experience the pop of the page.

Then you can encounter that flash of clarity Peter had when he recognized the true identity of Christ, and Jesus told him, "Flesh and blood did not reveal this to you, but My Father who is in heaven" (Matthew 16:17).

Then you can identify with the two disciples who walked

miles along the road to Emmaus, unaware that they were in the company of the resurrected Jesus. Suddenly their eyes were opened, they recognized Him, and they were awakened by the Word. These disciples gave the perfect description of the pop: "Were not our hearts burning within us while He was speaking to us on the road, while He was explaining the Scriptures to us?" (Luke 24:32). Our cold, confused hearts—when moved by the Word—burn with love. This is the pop. Our spirit is awakened, life is engaged, and the heart becomes tender and transformed.

As you read, pray for an Emmaus road moment.

Now that we have discovered the way of the ear and some general principles for reading Scripture, it is time we embark on the process of discovering your life verse.

PART IV

UNI-VERSE: DISCOVERING YOUR LIFE VERSE

I SAT AT DINNER with one of my best friends, and he told me of his journey in discovering his life verse:

> My life was full of anxiety. I was upset, scared, and stressed out. I was popping prescription pills throughout the day, at the office, at home. Often in traffic I found myself weaving in and out of traffic-jammed lanes yelling at other drivers because they were going to make me late for my yoga class. The counselor I was seeing told me my anxiety came from not dealing with my true emotional needs.
>
> My life had become a series of negative thoughts, which had grown and multiplied to capture virtually every thought. I felt so miserable. My life circumstances weren't bad. I had a successful medical practice, a loving

wife, great kids, and two really fast sports cars. But disappointment and self-pity took root in my mind.

I was living with a multitude of dramatic impulses, including cheating, lying, being stalked, enabling, ruining happy moments, competing, manipulating, betrayal by longtime friends, and chronic depression. I felt jealousy, guilt, rage, grief, shame, loss, hopelessness. I was emotionally frozen and despondent, never able to be real. I frequently swore off bad habits, only to turn to the world of drugs. I was in a downward spiral. I sabotaged my career and forgot the people in my life who loved me. And that was on a good day. I had stopped living. I felt blocked and worn out. The story I was living was killing me.

I had always believed in God, but I had kept Him in the background. I believed the Bible was the Word of God, but I wasn't well acquainted with it. All I knew was what I picked up from listening to Sunday sermons. I was a man without a verse.

In my days off I began to read for myself. Not long after that I read a verse that changed my whole perspective. "Do not be conformed to this world, but be transformed by the renewing of your mind" (Romans 12:2). With those words bouncing in my thoughts, I began to have new thoughts. *Maybe I don't have to be angry, afraid, hurt. Maybe I don't have to live with a spirit of blame.*

The power of Scripture in my life cut through

all my defenses and catapulted me into change. The death grip of my old way of thinking was broken. At that point I began to have a new perspective. My life verse is my go-to passage for all my endeavors.

My friend's story is a reminder that where there's a verse, there is life.

✦   ✦   ✦

You're not alone. Others would enjoy hearing how you discovered your life verse and the difference it has made for you. Visit YourLifeVerse.org and share.

CHAPTER 12

Anatomy of a Life Verse

GOD'S WORD has staying power. The same can't be said for everything. Some things wear out, others rust out, while still others go in and out of style. Late-night television is filled with commercials promising that their gimmicky products will make life better, faster, and stronger. Chairs you hang upside down to take away back pain. It's true: After only minutes being inverted 180 degrees, all feeling in the body is gone. There are blenders to grind up all your food, because it's easier to drink from a cup than to cut food with a knife. And I do appreciate when they put the food commercials before the exercise commercials—their way of saying, "This is how you gain, and this is how you lose."

But for all the overblown promises and hype, where are they now? Faded into the dust of the airwaves. Things wear out. They lose their appeal. Anyone who has driven past a junkyard has seen once-beautiful cars that were some-one's object of desire, now discarded, piled up in heaps and used for spare parts. All of man's inventions—bought, owned, or longed for—will eventually see their end. All our attempts to find meaning and worth will pass away. Everything connected to us humans eventually ends. This is the point Isaiah makes: "The grass withers, the flower fades, but the word of our God stands forever" (Isaiah 40:8). All the world with its quick fixes is as fragile as grass and as weak as a flower. A life spent self-authoring our stories has an empty, unsatisfying ending. But the words of God stand the test of time.

Sounds good, doesn't it? There is, however, a problem. How does the Word of God last forever? As I write this chapter from my study, on a shelf behind me I have a stack of Bibles from which I've preached for the last twenty years. All of them are weathered from repeated use in various climates and settings. The covers are tattered, the spines are broken, the pages are falling out. Some are ripped and have been taped, while most of the pages are yellowed from the sun and track lights. There are highlighter stains where colors have bled through from one page to the next. The margins are inked with sermon notes. Favorite verses bear tear stains from moments when those words have popped off the page, when I needed them the most.

These books are in a state of decay. No doubt they will not last forever. But there is something buried there between the covers, something beyond the ink and paper: the Word of God.

A friend of mine is building a new house. It's a beautiful mix of old-world and modern, and one day he was giving me a tour, taking me from room to room to point out the unique features. We were walking in the garage when he asked if I'd noticed the floor.

"Yes, of course," I said, thinking he was referring to the flagstone throughout the house.

"No," he said, "this floor." He pointed down to the garage floor, sweeping aside construction dust with his shoe. "It's crushed glass and stone. These sparkling stones were ground down to fit neatly together. Once the dust is gone, it will be polished to a high gloss."

We had been talking while walking the length of the garage, and after he pointed it out, I could see that this floor was going to be stunning. I'd had no idea what I was standing on.

The same is true with reading Scripture—we are standing on jewels and precious stones, which go unnoticed until we slow our reading. The words get covered in the dust from speeding through the text. Slowing our reading brings benefits, helping us submit to the text.

Active Steps on the Quest

Among the jewels you will find in Scripture—if you read slowly, openly, submissively—is your life verse. Robert Noland, a friend of mine, is a gifted musician, writer, and speaker. He and I were attending a writers' think tank, and during one of the breaks I asked him if he had a life verse. He told me his story:

I heard the gospel for the first time at age twelve and accepted Christ as my Savior, but I was never discipled and grew up in a Christian-neutral home (not for or against, just indifferent). About six months out of high school, I went on a church trip after having been away from fellowship for six years. That week, I got it. I saw it. I experienced it. I realized there was a lifestyle that Jesus calls us to. I repented. I turned away from the world and toward Him.

I began reading God's Word, and it was transforming my mind. In one of those early Bible reading sessions, I was in 2 Corinthians. As I read through chapter 5 in my NIV, a verse leaped off the page, went deep into my heart, and sent ripples out into my future. Verse 17: "Therefore, if anyone is in Christ, he is a new creation; the old has gone, the new has come!"

Regardless of the version in which you read this verse, the heart and spirit of it are obvious. Christ has changed everything. Life as you know it will never be the same.

I loved everything about that verse. It was the gospel in a nutshell. It was God's offer to all mankind with the promise of what He will do. And for me it wrote my biography in a single sentence. You want to know what my life is about? Second Corinthians 5:17 says it all.

Most people I interviewed about finding their life verse couldn't remember how they had found it. Some simply adopted a verse their friends were using.

I've always heard when you stop looking for love, that's when you find it. But since when does anyone find anything by *not* looking for it? Jesus told a parable about a shepherd who left ninety-nine sheep to find the missing one, and so far I've not seen a revised version where the shepherd stops looking. The parable of the pearl of great price tells of a man who discovered a treasure and sold all he had to obtain it. There's no updated version where the man stands around shouting, "I'm gonna stop looking now!" followed by the pearl rolling to his feet. The father of the prodigal son never stopped looking; he had a positive expectancy that his lost son would return, and even ran to meet him and bring him home.

In every case in the parables, when something is lost, someone goes looking in the right way and in the right places. You can't discover your life verse by standing around and hoping you hear somebody else quote a verse that sounds cool. For most, the struggle in discovering their life verses has to do with not knowing where in the Bible to start reading. I've developed a process that is simple and easy to apply.

Locate Your Life

Every place your life has taken you has one common denominator: you. Like it or not, you are the person you've spent the most time with. You are the one you've invested the most in. Yet for all the life you've lived up to now, you might be the one you know the least about.

You are unique, with your own set of skills, talents, and abilities. There will never be another you. For you to come and go without being connected to God would be tragic.

Knowing where to find your life verse begins with locating your life, and that will take radical honesty on your part. Because of the work of Jesus, your death sentence has been disarmed so you no longer have to live out the old story. Locating your life starts with you being your real self in the presence of God. It can be one of the most constructive and rewarding journeys of your life.

To get into a place of honesty, begin by praying this psalm:

Search me, O God, and know my heart; test me and know my anxious thoughts. Point out anything in me that offends you, and lead me along the path of everlasting life. (Psalm 139:23-24, NLT)

Contemplate the big picture of your life. Contemplation is not about contorting your body into a figure eight and chanting, nor does it involve dressing hip, carrying a leather journal, and drinking overpriced coffee. It's about reflecting on the way of your life and learning to be led along the path of life.

Can you see Isaac in Genesis 24:63 going out into the field to meditate? He was reflecting on his past, present, and future, getting a clear picture of his life. Jesus went into the desert for forty days and faced rigorous inventory of His life. Upon returning to the synagogue, He knew where to locate His life verse. Later in His ministry He would express His life verse using a variety of images: *I'm the way, the truth, the life, the light, the vine, the good shepherd.* He was a powerful example of the clarity that locating your life brings.

The exercise of locating your life may involve journaling (or any other mode of expression—painting, drawing, sculpture, dance), or you might simply mentally store away the memories and patterns that emerge. However you do it, it should prepare you for the next step in contemplating the big picture of your life.

Inventory Your Life

Take as much time as you need to think slowly through the following questions, letting the Spirit guide you through finding the answers.

List your top five positive, life-shaping events. Keep in mind that a life-shaping event is not always a major moment; it can be something small that leaves a mark on you.

Now list the top five negative events of your life.

What made these events so profound for you? This is where you'll need the help of the Spirit.

As you look back, it's important to remember that these events—both positive and negative—shaped your thinking and may have even been the source of a death sentence you carried with you through life.

As you think about these ten life-shaping events, move on to this next question:

What theme do all these events have in common? Choose one of the themes listed below. Life is not always pleasant, and the themes of the sum total of our lives are not always positive. Circle the one that applies to you:

> *Freedom*
> *Trust*
> *Hurt*
> *Hope*
> *Love*
> *Encouragement*
> *Presence*

The theme you've just chosen will help considerably in narrowing your search for your life verse, as I'll explain next.

CHAPTER 13

Roaming the Neighborhood

SPENDING TIME with God happens differently for each of us. Some find that regular liturgy heightens the celebration of God along ancient paths, while others prefer a comfortable chair surrounded by a peaceful atmosphere of music and candles. Some like to journal, others kneel in a quiet place. Whatever the means, the objective of the spiritual disciplines is to move us toward connecting with God's presence.

For me, it's walking. After reading Scripture, I like to get out, walk, and let God's words marinate. As I walk, I imagine all the distractions and irritations cluttering my heart and my mind being swept off me by the breeze. I do some of my best thinking when I walk.

Long walks help me assimilate the words I've been reading. The long distance, the quietness, the solitude, the varying textures of the grass or pavement under my feet—all help my mind and body participate with the work of the Spirit. As I stride in rhythm, putting one foot in front of the other, simple truths of Scripture are validated and new thoughts are confirmed.

One crisp fall morning, walking through my neighborhood, I was replaying a conversation with a friend of mine. The day before, we were standing in the parking lot of a local trendy restaurant when our conversation turned to the topic of the Bible. I mentioned I'd been working on a talk about it when he said, "Oh, I need to hear that! You know, I pick up my Bible, open it, look at it, and think, *Eh, I don't get it.*"

I found his honesty refreshing. Because after years of studying the Scriptures, I still sometimes have the same thought. Feeling the brisk air cut through my clothes, I continued to walk and pictured my desk, still stacked with various translations of the Bible, commentaries, and other tools for understanding. All this, and I still I have moments of *Eh*.

Echoing in my heart were the words of David found in Psalm 19:7-8,10-11:

> The law of the LORD is perfect, restoring the soul;
> the testimony of the LORD is sure, making wise the
> simple. The precepts of the LORD are right, rejoicing
> the heart; the commandment of the LORD is pure,
> enlightening the eyes. . . . They are more desirable
> than gold, yes, than much fine gold; sweeter also
> than honey and the drippings of the honeycomb.
> Moreover, by them Your servant is warned; in
> keeping them there is great reward.

These words were born in the heart of David out of long hours of success and failure, through seasons reigning as king and on the run as a fugitive. As I was moving through the streets of my neighborhood, my present thoughts intertwined with the past, and I imagined David intently, slowly, like an expert tailor working quietly through the night, meticulously weaving words about the Word.

David enjoyed the Word of God. Consider David's loving attention to detail, his deep love for God, the many ways the Word of God sustained him through his life. These are astounding. But even more impressive was the *source* of inspiration for David's expressions of his love for God's Word. He didn't have a Bible like ours, filled with textual notes and commentaries on nuances of words. David was reading Torah, the Law—the first five books of the Bible, including Leviticus and Numbers, spilling over with laws, rules, and regulations. Yet David calls this "sweeter than honey." Through Torah he gained insight into the heart of God.

Maybe the problem is not with Scripture—perhaps we are too uptight in our approach. Rigidity kills responsiveness. My friend in the parking lot that day perceived the Bible as a giant task, a mountain to be climbed. Reading should be less attack, less taking on the sixty-six books, less trying to get through it . . . and more like a delightful stroll.

I felt a stirring in my heart and mind, usually a strong indicator of a lesson to be learned. I became more aware of my surroundings and noticed the different houses lining the streets—a blend of contemporary brick-and-rock or old-world stone built right next to each other on lots of varying sizes, the row bending down the road.

Reading Scripture should be like walking through a neighborhood. My neighborhood is named after a flower native to Oklahoma and includes four subdivisions: garden homes, villas, family homes, and estates, each meeting a different need in its unique way.

In every city, when learning your way around, you'll find there are so many neighborhoods that it's often hard to know just where to begin. Many people have the same feeling about finding their life verse, and this can be a major sticking point. Because of unfamiliarity with the Bible, many decide just to let it fall open and begin on whatever page it opens to. This is what I call Scripture roulette—a dangerous practice that removes Scripture from its context or "neighborhood." It would be odd to take a modest cottage from midtown Memphis and set it down next to a prewar high-rise in Manhattan, wouldn't it? In like manner, this is what happens when we blindly lift verses off the pages, extracting them out of the neighborhoods in which they were built. Our reading, while remaining relaxed and receptive, has to be more orderly than random selection.

Getting our bearings with Scripture begins by knowing the layout of the neighborhoods within the city. The Bible is comprised of sixty-six subdivisions (books) built within seven neighborhoods:

> *Law*
> *History*
> *Wisdom*

> *Prophecy*
> *Gospels with Acts*
> *Epistles*
> *Apocalypse*

Each subdivision and neighborhood is populated by people and their stories. Rulers, families, heroes, villains—many enjoyed wondrous intimacy with God, and they all weathered the storms of life. Each neighborhood was constructed during a particular period of time with its own worldview, culture, language, and customs. There are no ghettos in Scripture; each book offers a different perspective on life with God, and all were built in response to a need: our need to know God.

All of these neighborhoods have streets and addresses called chapters and verses. Like an address, the numbers provide greater ease for locating, dropping in, and listening to the stories.

The neighborhoods of Scripture provide multiple access points for discovering your life verse. By roaming, we find our personal places in the neighborhood. It's important to remember when roaming through the neighborhoods of the Bible: The goal is not to master the text but to discover God and, among other things, His life verse for you. Roaming means reading until you run into a verse that speaks directly to you, then hanging out there for a while.

The lesson I learned on my walk that day was one I want to pass on to my friend in the parking lot and to anyone who's ever felt frustrated at the thought of reading Scripture:

Lighten up.

Don't try so hard.

Just read until something pops off the page.

Finding your life verse involves knowing where to start reading in Scripture. In the last chapter, you circled one of seven words—the overarching theme of ten key events of your life. Your theme corresponds to a neighborhood of Scripture.

Following, I have provided a brief description of each neighborhood of Scripture, to help you understand the kinds of subdivisions (books) you'll be entering and to describe the manner in which each neighborhood addresses your theme. Please understand that my suggested one-word summaries of the seven Bible neighborhoods are greatly oversimplified but still helpful, especially if you're just getting started with Bible exploration. These seven words have been for me a devotional map to guide my reading, and I present them here as an imperfect but useful road map for locating the neighborhood in which your life verse might be found.

Freedom

The first five books make up the neighborhood of the Law (Genesis through Deuteronomy). They walk us through the story of the creation of the world, then how freedom was given to man and then lost through rebellion. They show us how God formed a people called Israel until, trapped in slavery, this infant nation cried out for help. God freed Israel, taking them from Egypt to the Promised Land. This neighborhood also contains the rules for living in celebration of God's presence. Rules that concerned thoughts, actions, choices, relationships, work, community life, and social order. These were not rules of legalism given by a score-keeping God; they were the means for people to break free from what had held them back.

For some, all of life has seemed to be a battle for freedom accompanied by a cry for help—a continual struggle between extremes: staying trapped versus being free. As you read these books, listen for your life verse to speak to the big picture of freedom. Regardless of the situation, God is your freedom-bringer.

Trust

The next neighborhood contains twelve Historical Books that track the journey of Israel from the time they entered the Promised Land, through the establishment of a kingdom, and beyond to its demise. The underlying theme of these books is trust. Joshua had to fully trust as he received the new role of leader from Moses. Then trust was broken when every man did what was right in his own eyes, and God sent a series of judges to call Israel back to trust. Ruth was a shining example of trust—the loss of her husband was shattering, but God turned it to good as she continued to place her trust in Him.

The middle books of history are each two volumes—Samuel, Kings, and Chronicles—and give a glimpse of the importance of trust. With Saul, trust was contaminated; he began well, but greed for power and wealth were his undoing. The last years of his reign were characterized by partial, then forsaken, trust in God. David demonstrated trust as a young shepherd of sheep, later becoming king and shepherd of people, always trusting God to deliver and guide him. Finally, Solomon illustrated trust compromised. Wealthy, wise, and powerful, he made many choices that weakened his trust in God.

The last three books in this neighborhood—Ezra, Nehemiah, Esther—show God raising up leaders to recast a vision of trust. We find the people of God morally distorted, socially disjointed, and economically bankrupt when God began a steady process of rebuilding their trust in Him.

As you read for your life verse in these books, let your prayer be, *Lord, lead me to trust.*

Hurt

Written in poetic form, the five books in this neighborhood amplify wisdom for the head and soul. Much of these writings were the journals and prayer books of people who experienced deep hurt, giving voice to the many cries of the heart within God's Word.

Job had had nothing but good days. At first. He was wealthy and walked with God, then unexpectedly, life disintegrated in crisis. Experiencing great misery, he continually asked God, *Do You hear me?* He found God in the messes of life. There are no easy answers to explain the hurt we face, but like Job, we call out to God and hear through the hurt.

The Psalms held a permanent place in the life of Israel, providing them with a vehicle to approach God with extreme honesty, expressing a wide variety of hurts and laments, as well as renewed confidence in God. In being honest about the hurt, we find a God who helps, who speaks verses of life to Israel. And we're inspired to stand unflinchingly in the face of hurt.

The writers of Proverbs sought God as they figured out life day by day, dealing with the details and demands of life. So this book overflows with every imaginable situation humans face. And in Ecclesiastes, Solomon in his search for wisdom was crying out to be heard by God.

If hurt has been your life's theme, God has a life verse for you in this neighborhood.

Hope

This neighborhood contains the books of prophecy. Their role was to speak the heart of God to people in varying stages of moral decay, exile, captivity, and oppression, usually coming back around to a message of radical repentance and restoration. All sixteen of these prophets stayed on message, constantly pointing people toward God, faithfully communicating one simple truth: There is always hope. God had not forgotten them and was in faithful pursuit of them, seeking a personal relationship.

These books come in two varieties—major and minor— which indicate only the sizes of the books, not the importance of their messages. The major prophets—Isaiah, Jeremiah, Ezekiel, Daniel—proclaim that God *will* deliver; the minor prophets proclaim *the way* God will do it; both of them present the hope of change.

The thought of roaming through these seventeen

prophetic books may seem complex at first, but don't get bogged down in the details. Instead, listen for the heart of the prophet and the heart of the God for whom he spoke. There is hope in God's passionate love, in God's desire to live in our lives with faithfulness and intimacy.

Love

The four books known as the Gospels—Matthew, Mark, Luke, John—reveal different aspects of Jesus. When combined, they create a portrait which is both accessible and personal. Jesus is God with us. The Gospels bring us face to face with His person and teachings—jarring to the comfort of life, awakening the soul to real love. Jesus' parables and sermons are the catalysts of His kingdom.

Sure, His ministry made the sick well and brought the dead to life. But when people were near Jesus, even more happened—they felt loved. Normal, everyday people met authentic love. Nicodemus found unconditional love and acceptance that religion could never offer him. The Samaritan woman was the subject of much gossip, but Jesus never judged her. He spoke patiently and kindly, and the eyes of her heart were opened—she'd found the Savior.

There was also the woman taken in the act of sin, caught by religious leaders who encircled her with stones in hand, ready to pass judgment. But Jesus rescued her and showed that His new commandment was greater than the commands written in stone. Love had won.

Jesus ate with His disciples, His twelve closest friends, and then, wrapping a towel around his waist and taking a bowl of water, He went to each disciple and washed his feet. The task of a slave. He demonstrated intense commitment, real love.

And then, in His final act of love, He took on the sin of humanity.

Have you lost love? Never been loved for real? For some, life is filled with imitation love, a love that's conditional, based on behavior. Maybe you've been searching for real love your whole life. If love is the theme of your life, then as you roam this neighborhood with Jesus, listen for His true love—perfect love that casts out fear.

After the Gospels comes the book of Acts, revealing the history of the church's beginning. Commissioned by the risen Lord, the first Christ-followers were confident and clear about their message. Acts records the many ways they fearlessly spoke, lived, and demonstrated Christ's message and ministry. Through the help of the Spirit, anyone anywhere could experience the love of God.

You may have always believed in the fearless love of God but never known how to express it. Read and roam through this book and stay alert to what the Spirit has to say to you.

Encouragement

Of the New Testament neighborhoods, this is the largest—twenty-one letters written to churches and individual believers who were new in the faith. Paul is traditionally considered the writer of most of these, from Romans to Philemon, while various others wrote Hebrews to Jude.

The unifying theme of all the letters is encouragement.

These Spirit-inspired writers encouraged this new community of faith to believe all God had to say about them, to let go of what was hurting them, to stay in agreement with God, and to live free in the life of Christ. They were exhorted to know their position in Christ and to deepen their belief that in Jesus, they were accepted, appointed, and acquitted.

There is encouragement for you in these letters today. These books are not made up of clever self-help tricks, but rather provide a roadway to being spiritually alive. Whether you've always been in need of encouragement or have always had enough, either way it's good to know what God has to say about your life. Commit to taking your time to roam through these books. Be encouraged—this neighborhood houses some great potential life verses.

Presence

The New Testament closes with Revelation, a letter from John written during some dark days for Christians. Some of Jesus' last words on earth were, "I will always be with you," but the Christians living in Rome during the days of persecution probably didn't feel as if Jesus was with them; they felt abandoned. "Have you left us?" they cried.

John received Jesus' answer in three unforgettable encounters with the living Son of God. Jesus assured John in *person* that His people weren't forgotten. Further, John was astonished by Jesus' *performance*—He is the first and the last, alive forevermore. Finally John was affirmed by Jesus' *presence*. John had been exiled on the island of Patmos, separated from friends and family, but now Jesus stood before him and he knew he was not alone.

The point of this book is not that you'll be left behind but that you won't be left alone. Revelation is a tricky book to read, with unfamiliar imagery and multiple references to the Old Testament. But roaming doesn't require that you understand every detail.

If you've ever felt like you were alone, even in a crowd, or if you've always had the sense you didn't belong or didn't fit in, then your life verse might be here. There may be a verse or a line that puts life into perspective for you. Get ready, read, and pray.

Rules for Roaming

After you've picked a neighborhood, get your pen and a high-lighter and begin roaming through the first subdivision (the first book). An appropriate rhythm for this kind of reading is to roam and rest. Make yourself ready, take your time—remember you're strolling not stomping—and be receptive to what you're reading. Listen for the voice of the Spirit, your tour guide, to draw your attention to words or phrases. And when a verse pops off the page, take a moment to think about it. Let it trigger your imagination and emotions. Be open to any thoughts or memories you associate with that verse.

At this point, use your pen and pad to record those thoughts, memories, and insights. Ask God why you're drawn to this verse. Take time to listen and wait. Don't edit your thoughts, just think and talk with God, honestly and openly.

Now rest. Sit quietly and be present with God. If this is a struggle, imagine God speaking the verse over you. Now continue reading and roaming, letting what you read change you.

I've often found it helpful to read through an entire passage once out loud. By reading out loud, I experience the words as I form and speak them and understand meanings more clearly. I follow with a second reading, but this time silently, using a highlighter to mark passages that seem to be speaking to me. Finally, I go back through a third time, reading only the highlighted verses to see if any words pop off the page.

This may be enough guidance to help you find your life verse. Or maybe you still have questions. Let me see if I can answer a few of them . . .

CHAPTER 14

Taking the Life Verse Journey

THE OTHER DAY I was walking through a neighborhood when I spotted a house with a For Sale sign. Attached to the sign was a plastic box filled with fliers yelling about the property. On a whim, I took a flier to read as I continued my stroll through the neighborhood. At the top of the page was a picture, followed by stats about the house. But the closing point nearly did me in: "This house is nestled in an interior lot in a sought-after neighborhood."

This place was within walking distance of my hotel, which was located near a major highway. I guess if you like falling asleep to semis, sirens, and the whooshing of traffic, then this is the place. This "interior lot" was crammed between two other houses with only enough room for a garbage can between them. This "sought-after neighborhood" had seen its best days twenty-five years ago.

What I learned that day on my walk was that people don't always mean what they say. These fliers need some decoding.

> *"Nestled" means cramped.*
> *If it's "charming," it's in need of repair.*
> *"Quaint" means tiny, and "spacious" means even tinier.*
> *When a house is described as "airy," it means the north wind blows through the cracks in the wall.*
> *"Must see to appreciate" is a beautiful way of saying the house has been condemned.*
> *"A view of the water" means the neighbors' backed-up septic tank is within eyeshot.*

God isn't like that. When God speaks His Word to us through Scripture, He's not saying one thing and meaning another. Rather, what is on the page is uncovered, the truth brought out into the open.

That said, you may still be left with a question or two about how this life verse thing works. I'll try to address a few:

What If I Find More Than One Possible Life Verse?
Many of these neighborhoods and subdivisions have many chapters and verses, so it's possible, as you roam through these areas, you might run across multiple verses that speak to you. Mark each of them and plan to circle back to reread them. Should you happen to compile a number of verses, here are some ways to evaluate them.

You might find verses that have good thoughts or that challenge you to think, but your life verse should contain passion, and a sense that God has filled this verse with special purpose for you. If a particular verse doesn't, you should still keep it in mind for further study.

Your life verse should inspire positive action that will make an eternal difference in your future.

A common characteristic of a life verse is that it will help you influence others in God-honoring ways.

Consider also these questions:

> *How do you react to this verse upon first discovery? One week later?*

> *Does this verse awaken something new inside you?*

> *Does it provide clarity regarding the way you've been living?*

> *Does it stretch you to make adjustments in the way you're living?*

> *Does it fit you?*

> *Do you have to trust God to live it?*

> *How does your verse relate to your talents or spiritual gifts?*

What If I Pick the Wrong One?

You can't be wrong when it comes to believing in God's Word! Many people I talk to don't have a life verse at all, and having *any* verse is better than having none. Whatever verse speaks to you, it's much better than living by a death sentence. Once you set yourself on the journey of roaming the scriptural neighborhood, you'll be guided, as long as you stay focused on God and dependent on the Spirit.

Can I Change My Life Verse?

There are no unbreakable rules here, but I would ask, Why would you need to change? It's called a life verse because it involves your whole life. Certainly all of the Bible is meant as God's message to each of His children, and as you read it throughout your life, you should find new portions speaking to you in new ways. But I believe that each person can discover one verse in particular that serves as a frame for all of the others, bringing all of your life's discoveries in Scripture into unity.

As time goes on, you may discover new meaning and application in your life verse. My life verse has always been Deuteronomy 23:5. What that verse meant to me when I discovered it at sixteen is different from the way that I see it now. That verse has been battle born, tried, and tested. It's been well used and, like most quality things, has gotten better with time. To this day I continue to find new insight and application in that verse. The words of Deuteronomy point me to a Savior who is not just concerned with exercising His might but who is personally, compassionately involved in the events of my life.

I recommend that you stay with your verse, do life with it, learn from it. Listen to it speak to you in all the different ages, stages, and seasons of life.

Can I Have Someone Else's Life Verse?

I understand how this happens. You hear a sermon or a testimony, someone quotes a verse, and you think, *Oh, that's good. I want that verse!* This is what I call "life verse envy." As I recall, we are not to covet. Working through the process of discovering your verse makes the one for you pop off the page and speak to you. (If, after you've discovered your life verse through this process, it ends up being the same as someone else's, that's great. After all, there are only so many verses in the Bible.)

Checking the Verse

A life verse should be inspiring, clear, and engaging. Your verse will impact your talents and interests, helping you understand better how they serve your life purpose. When Jesus read His life verse out of Isaiah 61, it painted a picture with new, specific direction, and it encompassed His whole life. When He personalized it by saying, "Today this Scripture has been fulfilled," it created an uproar. Don't expect everyone to be pleased with the outcome in our life. As Jesus lived out His verse, He caused the old, performance-based religious system to be dismantled.

If you were to take your verse seriously, would it have the same effect on your life that Jesus' verse had on His? Giving clear direction, backed up with passion?

How does your verse connect to the rest of Scripture? List as many stories in Scripture as you can that illustrate your life verse.

Does your verse cause you to see Jesus more clearly? When you think about your life story, does this verse make you more aware of Him being present during the past and present seasons of your life?

Discovering your life verse may take some time and persistence, "trying on" different possible verses until God's chosen verse finds you. Once you have discovered your life verse, you begin a new journey, putting it into practice. There is a pattern in the lives of the people in Scripture who lived according to their life verse. They read, believed, and lived out their verses. Their words and their lives were expressions of the Word God had spoken to them. So now it is time to amplify your verse with the voice of your life.

Exploring and Amplifying Your Life Verse

Now that you've discovered your life verse, it's time to explore it. The following is a series of exercises and questions to give you a fuller, more complete understanding of your life verse and its practical implications for you.

First, on a separate sheet of paper in the back of this book, write your life verse four times, each time using a different translation. This helps you gain more insights you might not have noticed with one reading.

Now rewrite your life verse in your own words to make your verse more personal.

Write your verse in present tense and place your name in it.

Write your verse in the form of a prayer.

Take some time to explore your life verse in light of the rest of Scripture. Answering these questions will help you to discover how your verse is connected to the rest of Scripture.

Is your verse repeated in Scripture? Where? (If you have a Bible containing Scripture references in the margin, begin there by looking up each reference to notice if the verse is directly quoted or referred to in part.)

Go back to your original life theme you chose before you began reading (one of the seven words summarizing the seven neighborhoods of Scripture). *Use a concordance to look up that theme word (and related words) to see where it appears in Scripture.*

What stories in Scripture illustrate your verse? (Look for specific stories in both Testaments.)

Evaluate Your Life Verse
Does it summarize your whole life? Please explain.

Write a brief summary about how your verse applies to each of the following areas. Over time your answers will become statements of your belief, of how the truth of your verse affects these five major areas.

Personal

Professional

Relationships

Family

Financial

How does your life verse change the way you see the resources you have available in your life?

How would your dealings with others change if you believed the message of your life verse?

How does this verse encourage you in terms of your whole life's purpose and direction?

Enhance Your Life Verse

Think about the tension in your life verse.

What most excites you about the verse?

What's most disturbing to you about the verse?

What one lesson could you teach from this verse?

Examine Your Life Verse

Answering these basic but essential questions is beneficial to examining the content of your life verse. In every life verse there are three components to investigate:

Potential
> *List the promises contained in your verse.*

> *How many positive ways does this verse impact your life?*

Problems
> *Specify any personal obstacles that make it hard for you to believe this verse.*

> *Name any personal fears that create a barrier to trusting God fully.*

> *What struggles and problems will you encounter because of this verse?*

Procedure
> *What procedure would you have to follow to live out this verse?*

> *What actions or choices does your verse ask of you?*

Experience Your Life Verse

The effectiveness of your life verse is all in how you take it. There are only two possible responses to your life verse: fear or faith. *On a scale of one (fear) to ten (faith), which one of the two do you feel the most? Please explain.*

Finally, I'd be grateful if you'd visit YourLifeVerse.org and share your life verse story—how it found you, how it changed you, how it continues to challenge you.

As you've answered these questions, perhaps you've found your world and your sense of eternity opening up and expanding with possibilities. Keep your attitude of openness to God's direction now as we talk about a few more aspects of living with your life verse.

CHAPTER 15

Living with
Your Life Verse

ONE OF THE MOST IMPORTANT aspects of the journey is learning to live with your life verse. After all, your life verse is
God's to use in your life, not yours to do with as you choose.
In the past, we put ourselves at the center of the story, but
that me-centric arrangement didn't go so well. Now we are
in God's story; He is at the center, and it's a different and
better way of living.

The way of the Word is to learn how your verse changes
your story, then begin to live into it. This is what it's like to
grow up into God's world. There's a period of time when we
have to unlearn our old story and reorient ourselves to live
as God's own in God's world. We give the Bible a beatdown
if we use our life verse just for what it can do for us, or as an
amenity to add flair to our old way of living.

Something far more grand is going on with your life verse.

Engaging the text of your life verse enables you to stop trying to find God in your story, and instead find your story in God.

Abraham, Moses, and David knew how to live with their life verses. They learned that it's a multidimensional, constantly evolving, ever-challenging experience. It ain't easy.

One dimension of living with your life verse is the discipline to be faithful when circumstances go against you. This is not a super-spiritual, hyper-religious exercise, but a means by which your life verse and the promise it holds are guarded. Hit hard by life, we tend to doubt and to think, *One verse—really? Won't I outlive it or find it to be irrelevant? Isn't there a danger that it won't work or might force me into a way of living that's restrictive?*

But when we think this, we're forgetting that without God, our story was always small, while the world of God's Word is gigantic. Scripture opens a world that is amazingly large and operates on God's heartbeat, His desires, and revelation of Himself. When we explore His world, we attain to insight that brings us out of the sin-ridden junk of ourselves.

Living with your life verse will at times cause you to have to seek clarity about the promise He's given you. You'll need to be ever vigilant to avoid drifting back into your old story. The present challenge is to live with your life verse and let it work. Deepen your certainty of the verse you've been given.

You are not at the center of the story; you are not in charge of transforming yourself. Thankfully you grow with your growing understanding of the Word that's been revealed to you by the Spirit. Every time you say, "God, I believe this," you are moved deeper into His story.

Your Life Verse Follows a Specific Promise

All Abraham ever had to go on was the promise of God. Abraham had come from a family of idol worshippers, which made him a total outsider when it came to the presence and the ways of the true God. Still, God had spoken to him, and Abraham's faith response to God's direction resulted in a personal and spiritual relationship with God. He believed the Lord. Abraham displayed great confidence in the promise he had received from God and went in obedience to the land of Canaan, even at the cost of leaving his relatives and the world that was familiar to him.

Abraham's friendship with God deepened until, twenty-five years after his departure from his original homeland, Abraham received a promise of a son whose descendants would be as numberless as the stars:

> The word of the LORD came to him, saying, . . . "One who will come forth from your own body, he shall be your heir." (Genesis 15:4)

This was Abraham's life verse, promising a future life that would extend beyond him. This promise was followed by years of waiting to see it fulfilled. This was a time of struggle as both Abraham and his wife aged frighteningly closer to a century each. Abraham endured feelings of uncertainty about the promise, along with the desire to take back control from his life verse. But God was as good as His Word, and the promised heir, Isaac, was born when Abraham was one hundred.

After many more years had passed, Abraham's loyalty to his life verse was once again tested:

> Take now your son, your only son, whom you love, Isaac, and go to the land of Moriah, and offer him there as a burnt offering. (Genesis 22:2)

Abraham willingly responded and did as the Lord said, with the Lord stepping in to preserve and bless Isaac. The backbone of Abraham's willingness was the life verse he had received from God long ago.

Your life verse has a promise within it. You must know the meaning along with the energy and spirit in which it's spoken. Its promise is the presence of God.

And then there was Moses. He was startled out of his quiet life as a shepherd in Midian when the angel of the Lord appeared to him in the flame of a burning bush and gave him his life verse:

> Come now, and I will send you to Pharaoh, so that you may bring My people, the sons of Israel, out of Egypt. (Exodus 3:10)

His every challenge and test, his every trial and struggle, would be based on this life verse. Moses was challenged to take on a large-scale deliverance, completing what he had failed to accomplish on a small scale forty years earlier. It's not surprising that his reply to God was, "Who am I, that I should do this thing?" But rather than letting old fears and failure interpret life, we must each let his or her life verse do the interpreting and the guiding and give us strength. The promise in Moses' life verse was the accompanying presence and power of God. Don't forget to pay attention to the One who has spoken your life verse.

God often spoke of the high regard he had for David, handpicked by the Lord Himself. David had come from humble and obscure means; when Samuel had arrived at Jesse's house to anoint a king to take the place of Saul, David was in the field tending sheep. Samuel had each of Jesse's sons brought forward, and God told him not to look at the outward appearance but for the heart of a king.

God passed up seven sons until all that was left was David. Jesse did not consider him to be a contender for monarch-elect. Then Samuel insisted that he see David. God told Samuel that David was His choice for king. David was anointed that day, and his life verse came to be:

And the Spirit of the LORD came mightily upon
David from that day forward. (1 Samuel 16:13)

What follows in Scripture is an extensive and impressive résumé of David's success as a military leader, a psalmist, a prophet, and a king. All the good that David accomplished from that moment forward was based on his life verse.

We will have success, along with our share of problems.

David certainly had his own crises to deal with. But the promise in your life verse is God Himself. Continuing to recognize this simple and clear truth is the challenge of living with your life verse. Each of us will face a struggle not to break faith with his or her life verse, never to allow it to become diminished or dulled by problems and doubts. We can be sustained by continually recognizing the empowering presence of God.

Looking at these three men, we see a pattern—a unifying principle—in the way God gives us each a life verse. Each of these men had one. Each was assigned a specific task with its own unique focus. Each had his own struggles and conflicts.

The one element they have in common is that God was with them.

That's the promise.

Whatever your assignment—whether you struggle, whether you succeed—God is present. He is there, living in your life verse.

Give Your Life Verse a Voice

Your life verse is not just about one text; it belongs to all of Scripture. We don't shape our lives by ripping random verses from the Bible that are to our liking, sewing together bits and pieces of Scripture. We aren't making a quilt. Our life verses fit into the bigger story that the Holy Spirit has been speaking throughout all Scripture. The story is our voice.

When faced with the test concerning his son, Isaac, Abraham was careful about what he said. He could've complained: "Well, I have to go up that mountain and kill him.

That figures—nothing ever works out for me. God is so weird. If I were in charge, I would be doing it differently. Woe is me. I'm not in charge, so I guess I'll do it anyway." All complaining does is disconnect us from Scripture, making us opponents of God.

Instead Abraham magnified his life verse:

We will worship and then we will come back.
(Genesis 22:5, NIV, emphasis added)

Notice that Abraham said nothing about killing Isaac. Abraham said, *we will come back*, meaning he was planning, in faith, to return with Isaac. This is so striking because it reveals Abraham's faith wasn't in Isaac or in himself but in the promise of God! Abraham didn't just know his life verse; he knew the God of the verse.

We have to let the Word give voice to our words. This means finding as many ways as we can to plug into the God of our life verse and turn up the volume.

Then there's Moses. He and the Israelites were out of Egypt when Pharaoh's army caught up in pursuit. If ever there was a time for Moses to amplify panic and doubt and defeat, this was it. But no:

Moses said to the people, "Do not fear! Stand by
and see the salvation of the LORD which He will
accomplish for you today; for the Egyptians whom
you have seen today, you will never see them again
forever." (Exodus 14:13)

Moses' confidence was the content of his life verse. When Moses said, "Do not fear," Israel was not an army and had no weapons for war. Moses was giving voice to his life verse!

Up to this point there was no victory in sight, no indication of a way through. But Moses' faith was not in the circumstances; instead he drew courage from the God of his life verse.

If we are to live with our life verses, we must stay in the Book. It's a matter of urgency that the focus of our lives be linked to our focus in the Scriptures.

> David said to Saul, "Let no man's heart fail
> on account of him; your servant will go and
> fight. . . . *The* LORD who delivered me from the
> paw of the lion and from the paw of the bear, *He*
> will deliver me from the hand of this Philistine."
> (1 Samuel 17:32,37, emphasis added)

It would have been so easy to top the hill, see hordes of your brothers staring at Goliath, and turn and go the other way. David could've said, "Hey, looks bad for you guys. Here's a sandwich. See you later!"

Instead, he said, "The Lord who delivered me from the wild animals will do it again." That confidence was not arrogance. No, it was based on his life verse! David knew he was destined to be king, so his verse made him fearless and gave him nerve. The promise so sustained him that he was willing to take on the impossible. He knew that Goliath could not deter him from his future, any more than the lion and bear that he had defeated as a young shepherd. David was operating from the promise of his life verse.

Many Philistines will rise up in your path, giants who'll try to derail and distract you. Grab on to your life verse and remember, when you face an obstacle, to say to yourself, "It's just another Goliath, another lion, another bear. God will deliver me."

And speaking of voicing, think of some ways you can work your life verse into your conversations. Possibly tell how you discovered it. Or quote it and explain why it has meant so much to you. I've found that others are often inspired, interested, and intrigued by the idea of having a life verse.

Give voice to your verse.

Let Your Life Verse Lead

These men lived in a time of uncertainty, chaos, and conflict. Each of them had opportunity to take the easy way out of their circumstances, but they chose to live with their life verses. Their life verses were sentences crafted from high-grade steel that gave them amazing brilliance mentally and a spirit of courage in danger. Don't discount the power of your life verse. These three didn't. They held on in dogged determination and saw results.

And in each case, that faith-based determination was followed by great results:

"Do not stretch out your hand against the lad, . . . for now I know that you fear God." . . . Abraham called the name of that place The LORD Will Provide. (Genesis 22:12,14)

Abraham was blessed because he did not hold back; he obeyed God. God gave Abraham offspring who would bless the whole earth. Lives would be changed as result of the faith of Abraham.

> The horses of Pharaoh with his chariots and his horsemen went into the sea, and the LORD brought back the waters of the sea on them, but the sons of Israel walked on dry land through the midst of the sea. (Exodus 15:19)

Moses held on to his life verse and experienced the saving power of God. God parted the waters and made way. Today Moses' life tells us that God is able to deliver.

> David prevailed over the Philistine with a sling and a stone. (1 Samuel 17:50)

The victory over Goliath resulted in even more victory, driving the invading Philistines all the way back to their land. All because David held fast to his life verse. When the "strong men" of Israel saw only defeat, David saw opportunity. Criticism and discouragement could not stop him.

Your verse joins you to the story of God—the One for whom nothing is impossible—pulling you into the truth that every verse is accompanied by the presence of God. Your life verse is for living life.

The Creative Outworkings of a Life Verse

During the writing of this book I met hundreds of people who were facing hardships, the loss of loved ones, the loss of homes and jobs. They shared their stories with tears, but also with strength, courage, and the ability to maintain great joy in spite of great struggle.

One of those people, Pamela, told me her story:

> I've always believed in God and His Word. My life
> verse is Psalm 46:1: "God is our refuge and strength,
> a very present help in trouble." These words have
> been with me my whole life. I'm well acquainted with
> those words; it's my psalm of hope. Whether life was
> in total upheaval, or breaking down, this verse has
> taught me to trust fearlessly. In 2000, I was diagnosed
> with melanoma, and I took refuge in Him and
> believed He reigned over everything, including all the
> trouble. This verse infused my heart, mind, and spirit
> with great strength. I survived, I am living, and I've
> had no other melanomas since then.

Pamela's story reiterates how a life verse works. To her, her verse is full of life, healing, and meaning. God's Word has the creative ability to turn life's negative battles into victories, causing positive expectancy and turning suffering into divine healing. Pulling opportunity from the jaws of defeat. Granting power to handle life's transitions responsibly. Placing our complaints and grievances in a right perspective. And heightening the glory of our great God to a fever pitch.

Second-Story Living

The discovery of your life verse doesn't end with the discovery itself, left on the page of Scripture highlighted in a favorite color. The life verse brings us into a whole new way of seeing life. As we have seen, the discovery of your life verse calls for a different relationship with the text. The text we *listen* to is not a guidebook, a set of doctrines, or directions for being moral. Neither is it a document stuck in the past. The book before us is *life*. The book opens us up to creative ways of living faithfully for God in this world.

Discovering the life verse calls us to participate in the Word we read—to own it, to practice it, to reenact it. The substance of the text—its promise, its doctrines, its potential to change a life story—emerges from the surface and is released in the present. Reality is recast according to the contents of God's verses.

Discovering your life verse means not just reading but *doing* the text. A life verse becomes active when it's received, embraced, and lived in this time of life. The life verse amplifies the gospel through our lives. A life verse has a voice of its own, distinct from our own, distinct from the old death sentence we vocalized for so long. Living the life verse means letting the voice of the text speak its rich, dramatic truth into our common life.

Recently I was in a very large, very spacious furniture store in North Carolina. There were escalators ascending to different levels and skywalks connecting buildings. So large was this store that it had printed directories for shoppers.

Maps are not my thing. I'd rather read Greek than read a

map. I inquired of one of the salespeople, "How many stories does this place have?"

"Three," he answered. "You gotta go up a level. The good stuff is on the second story."

The same is true of each of us. We are not buildings, but our lives contain multiple stories. We began with our old story, the one that helped us make sense of the world from childhood. This old story was filled with fears, flaws, and death sentences.

The second story is our new story, the one God writes. (The third story is heaven, but that's . . . another story.) Trading our old story for a new story places us in proximity to the promise and the heart of heaven. Maybe we lived on the first story so long that we've lived with a shortsighted view of what life can be. But as long as we draw breath, our life's outcome is not final.

Maybe it's time we go up a story, where all the good stuff is. We are called to give up our old stories, the ones that have shaped and distorted our view of ourselves and God. In the new story God is the main character and is the source of life-giving power, to which we are given full access. A life verse takes us up to the new, second story. It becomes the new focal point, the good news of our life.

A life verse asks us daily to reimagine, reexperience, and relive our lives in the power of the one who makes the promises. A life verse is there to remind us that God is alive, available, and active in our story. An active life verse is constantly retelling its truth in a variety of forms, always reshaping our present circumstances to work according to His will, always imaginatively changing our thoughts into redeemed thinking.

A life verse is there to remind us that God is always at work. The ripple effect of a life verse is that it continues to touch our lives in new ways. The life verse announces the outcome. With each new application we are challenged to think, explore, decide, and risk believing that the good stuff is living on a new story.